Test Yourself in

CONSTITUTIONAL & ADMINISTRATIVE LAW

Test Yourself in

CONSTITUTIONAL & ADMINISTRATIVE LAW

Martin Hannibal
BA, LLM, Barrister
&
Stephen Hardy, LLB

Series Editor: Adrian Keane, Barrister, Reader, ICSL

BLACKSTONE PRESS LIMITED

First published in Great Britain 1997 by Blackstone Press Limited,
9–15 Aldine Street, London W12 8AW. Telephone: 0181-740 2277

© M. Hannibal, S. Hardy, 1997

ISBN: 1 85431 631 1

British Library Cataloguing in Publication Data
A CIP catalogue record for this book is available from the British Library.

Typeset by Style Photosetting Limited, Mayfield, East Sussex
Printed by Bell and Bain Limited, Glasgow

All rights reserved. No part of this book may be reproduced or transmitted in any form or by any means, electronic or mechanical, including photocopying, recording, or any information storage or retrieval system without prior permission from the publisher.

CONTENTS

Introduction   1

A. The purpose of the multiple choice tests – B. The nature and format of the MCTs – C. MCTs – Popular misconceptions – D. Advice on taking the tests

MCT1 Constitutional Law   9

MCT2 Administrative Law   31

Appendix 1 – Answers to MCT1   54

Appendix 2 – Answers to MCT2   55

Appendix 3 – Note-form answers to MCT1   56

Appendix 4 – Note-form answers to MCT2   76

INTRODUCTION

PLEASE DO NOT ATTEMPT OR EVEN READ, THE MULTIPLE CHOICE TEST QUESTIONS CONTAINED IN THIS BOOK UNTIL YOU HAVE READ THIS INTRODUCTION!

A. THE PURPOSE OF THE MULTIPLE CHOICE TESTS

It must be rare, on opening a book and turning to its first page, to be greeted by . . . a command, albeit a polite command. However, there is a very good reason for such a command: that if you do embark upon testing yourself in constitutional and administrative law by using the MCTs in this book *before* you have read the following few pages on: (a) the purpose of the MCTs, (b) the nature and format of the MCTs, (c) popular misconceptions and (d) advice on taking the tests, then it is likely that you will simply defeat the purpose of this book.

The MCTs contained in this book have two purposes. The first is to enable you to test, with speed and accuracy, whether you have a sound working knowledge and comprehension of the main principles of law and the leading cases in constitutional and administrative law. The MCT questions used are directed at the general rules, the principal exceptions to those rules and the leading authorities. Wherever possible, they concentrate on the modern law and important decisions. They are not directed at narrow, antiquated, abstruse or esoteric points that a practitioner, or even a scholar, might properly need to look up and research. This explains why, as we shall see, each question has to be answered in only $2\frac{1}{2}$ minutes.

The second purpose is to enable you, after the test, to look at the answers which have been provided and to identify, with precision, your weaknesses and the gaps in your knowledge and understanding, so that you can revisit these areas and take appropriate remedial action.

B. THE NATURE AND FORMAT OF THE MCTs

This book contains two MCTs, MCT1 and MCT2, which together cover most subjects normally found in the syllabus for undergraduate courses in constitutional and administrative law.

Each of the MCTs comprises 60 questions, to be taken at one sitting. The 60 questions set have to be answered in no more than $2\frac{1}{2}$ hours. This means that if you divide the time equally between the questions, you will have 2 minutes and 30 seconds to answer each question.

Format

The questions in the MCTs contained in this book are always accompanied by four possible answers: [A], [B], [C] and [D]. You are required to select just one answer, the one that you think is correct/the best.

The questions often take the form of a factual problem and conclude with a specific question, such as 'On these facts, what is the most appropriate advice to give to the client?' or 'On these facts, which of the following rulings is the judge most likely to make?' Questions of this kind are designed to test whether you are able to recognise the law appropriate to the given facts and/or whether you are able to apply the law to the facts and thereby identify the correct outcome.

Other questions take the form of a number of legal propositions, only one of which is correct or, as the case may be, incorrect, or they ask about a specific point of law. Thus as to the former, the question may read, 'Which of the following propositions is correct?' or 'Which of the following propositions is INCORRECT?' As to the latter, the question may state a rule of law and then conclude, for example, 'Which of the following is NOT an exception to this general rule?' Questions of this kind are designed to test your knowledge of the law.

Some questions combine both a factual scenario and a choice of legal propositions so that, after setting out the facts, the question may read, for example, 'Which of the following best describes the principles which the court should apply to these facts?'

C. MCTs – POPULAR MISCONCEPTIONS

MCTs are easier than traditional examinations

This view tends to be expressed by those who have never attempted an MCT. Multiple choice tests are not easier – they are different. The experience of students who have taken MCTs, both at home and overseas, is that such tests are, in their own way, much more demanding than traditional examinations. There are three principal reasons for this.

First, MCTs typically cover the whole syllabus. If you have been brought up on conventional examinations and have adopted the 'question-spotting' approach, the MCT will obviously come as a very nasty shock!

Secondly, the MCT offers no scope for the student who would waffle. In conventional examinations, some students, unaware or not too sure of the correct answers, will hedge their bets, setting out at length all such seemingly relevant legal knowledge as they possess, but making no real effort to apply the law, simply skirting around the central issues with deliberate equivocation. There is no scope for such tactics in the MCT: faced with four competing answers, only one of which is correct, you must nail your colours to the mast.

Thirdly, there is the obvious pressure that comes from having to answer 60 questions at the rate of $2\frac{1}{2}$ minutes per question. This calls for the ability to analyse, digest and comprehend material at speed, before reaching a firm conclusion, only to move on to repeat the exercise in the next question, and so on.

MCT means multiple guess

It is perfectly accurate to say that if you attempt an MCT in which each question had four competing answers, then by the law of averages you *can* score 25%. Sensible students, however, do not approach MCTs in the same way that they approach the national lottery. In the real world, even if they did, it would be of little assistance – the passmark is usually more than double 25%! On the Bar Vocational Course, for example, a student who answers correctly 60% of all the questions set (in the MCT in civil evidence and procedure or criminal evidence and procedure), will achieve a bare pass and in many jurisdictions the percentage required to pass is much higher. Further information is given below on how to mark and rate your performance in the MCTs in this book.

MCTs are inferior to traditional tests and examinations

The validity of this criticism depends upon what one is seeking to test or examine. Obviously the MCT is not an appropriate tool to test oral legal skills such as advocacy or negotiation, just as it would be an inappropriate means of testing the practical skills of a pianist or an airline pilot. Equally, it cannot test your *creative* legal powers, whether in writing a legal essay or answering a legal problem (although it is interesting to note, in passing, that there is a high degree of correlation between student results in MCTs and in other forms of testing which do involve oral performances and creative written work). However, experience shows that the MCT is an excellent vehicle for testing, with accuracy, levels of knowledge and comprehension and the power of legal analysis, in particular the ability to recognise the law appropriate to any given set of facts, to apply that law, and thereby to identify the correct outcome.

MCTs cannot test the 'grey areas'

This is simply incorrect! For every 'grey area' question, there can be a suitably 'grey area' answer. For example, if on a particular point the authorities conflict, the correct answer may simply read, 'The authorities are in conflict on this point'. (Note, however, that such wording may also be used for an incorrect answer, i.e. in a question where the authorities are not in conflict at all.) Another possibility, in 'grey areas', is to build a question around the facts of an important reported case, thereby testing whether you know of, and have understood, that case. That said, it is certainly true that it can be more demanding to set good MCT questions on 'grey areas', and for this reason they tend to be avoided, unless they concern an important area of the law.

D. ADVICE ON TAKING THE TESTS

The purpose of the MCTs in this book is likely to be defeated unless you observe certain basic rules.

1. *Do not attempt an MCT until you have completed your studies in the subjects covered*

The MCTs in this book are designed to be taken only *after* you have completed your studies in the subject areas covered by the MCT in question and *before* you are formally examined in them.

2. *Take the MCT under examination conditions*

Make sure you will have an *uninterrupted* period of 2½ hours in which to complete *the whole test*. Also, remove from the room any relevant books or materials that you might be tempted to use. MCTs are to be taken without access to books and materials.

3. *Observe the time limit*

Observe the overall time limit of 2½ hours and try to spend no longer than an average of 2¼ minutes on each question. You will doubtless find that some of the questions can be answered in less time, whereas others require slightly more time – the questions vary in length and difficulty. However, the overall time limit reflects the standard of the MCT as a whole, and should not be exceeded.

4. *Read all four competing answers to each question before making a selection*

Whether a question is a problem-type question or a propositions-type one, you should *always* look at all four competing answers before making a selection. There are three good reasons for doing so.

First, an answer may refer to another answer or answers. For example, the question may set out a judge's ruling on a particular point of law, and conclude, 'Which of the following reasons could justify the judge's ruling?' [A] may then set out one reason and suggest that this *alone* could justify the ruling; [B] may set out a different reason and suggest that this *alone* could justify the ruling; and [C] may read, 'The reasons in both [A] and [B]'.

Secondly, even when you are relatively confident that you know the correct answer before you even look at the options on offer, and you are therefore tempted simply to select the 'correct' answer and to ignore the other answers, reading those other answers to check that they are indeed incorrect is the best way of confirming your initial selection.

Thirdly, there may well be occasions when you are unsure as to the correct answer. In these circumstances, it is often possible to identify the correct answer by the process of eliminating others which you know to be incorrect. Often you will find that the question-setter has included one answer which although somewhat plausible is clearly incorrect, and another which is also incorrect, although not quite so obviously, thereby reducing the effective choice from four to two – the two remaining answers will test whether you have understood the legal principle in question.

5. *Deem the question-setter infallible*

If your initial reaction, on reading a particular question and the four competing answers, is that you need more factual information before you can select the correct answer, or that there are two correct answers, or that the correct answer seems to have been omitted, quickly swallow your pride and re-read the question to see if there is something which you have missed or the importance of which you failed to take note on the first reading. If, having re-read the question and answers, you remain convinced that you need more information, or that there are two correct answers, or no correct answer, then select the answer which, in your opinion, gets nearest to being correct or is the best from which you have to make a choice.

6. *Mark your performance*

After you have completed each MCT – and preferably after a break of suitable length – you will want to mark your performance. You will find the correct answers to MCT1 and MCT2 listed in Appendix 1 and Appendix 2, respectively. Award yourself one mark for each question that you have answered correctly. If you have selected one of the other three answers to the question, you should *not* subtract a mark – you simply gain no mark for that question. You may then rate your overall performance according to the following table.

Number of questions answered correctly in MCT1/MCT2	Comment
0–35	A performance ranging from the awful to the weak. At best, on 35, you are showing insufficient knowledge and comprehension in over 40% of all subjects tested.
36–44	A performance ranging from one of bare competence to competence. You are showing insufficient knowledge and comprehension in 26–40% of all subjects tested.
45–53	A performance ranging from the competent to the very competent. You are showing insufficient knowledge and comprehension in 11–25% of all subjects tested.
54–60	A performance ranging from the very competent to the outstanding. You are showing insufficient knowledge and comprehension in only 10% or less of all subjects tested.

7. *Review your performance*

After you have marked your performance, take a break! You need to be fully refreshed before you embark upon the most important part of the exercise, namely the review of your performance by reference to the written answers to the questions of MCT1 and MCT2, which you will find in Appendix 3 and Appendix 4, respectively. Thorough review is important because it allows you to identify with precision the gaps in your knowledge and understanding of the law with a view to further work or revision.

Look at *all* of the written answers, not just those to the questions which you got wrong. By looking at the answers to the questions which you answered correctly, you will usually confirm your understanding of the law. Sometimes, however, you may discover that although your answer was in fact correct, your reasoning was defective. Equally, you need to know the reasons for the answers at which you could only make an inspired guess.

MCT1

[TIME LIMIT: 2½ HOURS]

CONSTITUTIONAL LAW

1. Consider the following statements about the nature of constitutions:

(i) A document having a special legal sanctity which sets out the framework and principal functions of the organs of government within the state and declares the principles by which those organs must operate.
(ii) A body of laws, customs and conventions that define the composition and powers of the organs of the state and that regulate the relations of the various state organs to one another and to the private citizen.

Which of these statements correctly defines the meaning of a constitution?

[A] The statement in (i) but not (ii).
[B] The statement in (ii) but not (i).
[C] The statement in both (i) and (ii).
[D] Neither statement (i) or (ii).

2. Which of the following propositions is correct?

[A] Britain does not have a constitution.
[B] The British constitution is not codified.
[C] The British constitution is unwritten.
[D] The British constitution is entrenched.

3. Which of the following characteristics is INCORRECTLY applied to Britain's constitutional arrangements?

[A] The British constitution is rigid.
[B] The British constitution is bicameral.
[C] The British constitution is unitary.
[D] The British constitution is flexible.

4. Which of the following sources of constitutional authority will NOT always be recognised and given effect to by the courts?

[A] Legislation.
[B] Constitutional Conventions.
[C] The Royal Prerogative.
[D] European Community law.

5. Consider the following statements of constitutional practice.

(i)   The monarch has an absolute discretion to withhold the royal assent to legislation.
(ii) The royal assent to legislation has not been withheld since 1704.
(iii) The monarch has complete discretion when appointing the Prime Minister.
(iv) The monarch invites the leader of the largest party in the Commons to be Prime Minister.

Which statements correctly identify the operation of constitutional conventions?

[A] The statements in (i) and (iii).
[B] The statements in (i) and (iv).
[C] The statements in (ii) and (iv).
[D] The statements in (ii) and (iii).

6. The Minister of Defence, concerned at the rising cost of paying compensation to householders whose homes have been damaged during military exercises, has introduced into Parliament the Military Training Damage Reparations Act 1995. The Act establishes a statutory compensation scheme which pays only 50% of the cost of repairs to damaged property. The new legislation, which has yet to be brought into force, is intended to replace the existing property compensation scheme, provided for under prerogative powers. The minister is now considering introducing the new compensation tariff, not by implementing the new legislation through a statutory instrument, but through the exercise of the prerogative itself.

Advise the minister on the legality of his actions.

[A] Its unlawful for the minister to introduce a new compensation scheme under the prerogative.
[B] The minister's proposal is lawful as he is carrying out the will of Parliament.
[C] The minister's action is lawful as the prerogative provides him with full legal authority.
[D] The minister's action is lawful because the courts will not intervene in the exercise of prerogative powers.

7. Dicey's theory of 'Parliamentary sovereignty' is one of the most enduring principles of British constitutional thought. Which of the following statements is INCORRECTLY attributed to Dicey?

[A] The Queen in Parliament has the right to make or unmake any law.
[B] Political sovereignty lies with the electorate.
[C] The power and jurisdiction of Parliament is so transcendant and absolute that it cannot be confined within any bounds.
[D] No person or body recognised by British law has the right to override or set aside Parliamentary legislation.

8. Which of the following is NOT considered to be a legal limitation on the doctrine of Parliamentary sovereignty?

[A] The Act of Union with Scotland (1707).
[B] The Statute of Westminster (1931).
[C] The European Convention of Human Rights (1950).
[D] The European Communities Act (1972).

9. Lucy is a store detective who in the course of her duties arrested David and Susan on suspicion of stealing 3 shirts from a major department store. In making a 'citizen's arrest' Lucy exercised powers under s. 24(5) of the Police and Criminal Evidence Act 1984. Susan, who was found in possession of the shirts, has been found guilty of theft. David, who has been acquitted, has commenced civil proceedings against Lucy for false imprisonment and assault and battery. How would you advise Lucy on the lawfulness of her actions when arresting David?

[A] David's arrest was lawful where Lucy can show she had 'reasonable grounds'.
[B] David's acquittal shows no offence was committed and no power of arrest existed.
[C] David's arrest was lawful provided Lucy can show an offence occurred albeit committed by Susan.
[D] David's arrest was lawful if Lucy can show she exercised the power of arrest contained in s. 24(7) of the Police and Criminal Evidence Act 1984 which provides much wider discretion to the arrestor.

10. Alex has been arrested under s. 24 of the Police and Criminal Evidence Act 1984 on suspicion of stealing 2 compact discs from the Mega Monster Music Store. The 'relevant time' of his arrival at the police station noted on his custody record is Saturday 6 p.m. Assuming that Alex has not been charged with any offence, what is the latest time must he be released from police custody?

[A] After 24 hours on Sunday at 6 p.m.
[B] After 36 hours on Monday at 6 a.m.
[C] After 72 hours on Tuesday 6 p.m.
[D] After 96 hours on Wednesday at 6 p.m.

11. David has been charged with affray contrary to s. 3 of the Public Order Act 1986. It is alleged that whilst he was being chased by 3 police officers he incited his Staffordshire Bull terrier to attack the officers. As a result of the incitement, 2 officers were bitten on the leg by the dog. Consider the following.

[A] The prosecution contends that ordering the dog to attack the officers, was sufficient to constitute a 'threat' as required by s. 3.
[B] David contends the offence of affray cannot be committed by words alone, i.e. his incitement of the dog to attack is insufficient.
[C] David contends the officers didn't 'fear for their personal safety' as required under s. 3 because they didn't believe the dog would attack them.
[D] The prosecution contend the true test under s. 3 is whether 'a person of reasonable firmness present at the scene would fear for their personal safety'.

Which statement is INCORRECT in relation to the prosecution of an offence under s. 3?

12. You represent Matt who has been charged with an offence under s. 1 of the Official Secrets Act 1911 of committing 'acts prejudicial to the safety or interests of the State'. It is alleged that in order to stop British forces becoming involved in the conflict in former Yugoslavia, he immobilised three Hercules transport aircraft to prevent them taking British troops to the war zone. His defence is that he was acting in the 'State's interest' to stop British troops from being killed. Which of the following tests of what amounts to the 'State's interest' under s. 1 will the court apply?

[A] The 'State's interest' as defined by the Crown.
[B] The 'State's interest' as defined by the organised community at large.
[C] The 'State's interest' as defined by the government.
[D] The 'State's interest' as defined by the defendant.

13. Which of the following limitations on freedom of expression is an example of subsequent restraint?

[A] Certificates issued by the British Board of Film Classification.
[B] An action for breach of confidentiality.
[C] A 'D' notice.
[D] An action for defamation.

14. One of the following four statements accurately reflects the Diceyan definition of the term 'convention'. Which one?

[A] Formal rules of our constitutional arrangements, unenforceable at law.
[B] Informal rules of our constitutional arrangements, enforceable at law.
[C] Understandings, habits, practices, customs, maxims and precepts, unenforceable by law.
[D] Understandings, habits, practices, customs, maxims and precepts, enforceable by law.

15. Which one of the following correctly lists examples of Constitutional Conventions?

[A] Appointment of the Prime Minister; dismissal of ministers; dissolution of Parliament; individual ministerial responsibility; Parliamentary privileges; and the Commonwealth.
[B] Appointment of ministers; dismissal of ministers; dissolution of Parliament; individual ministerial responsibility; and the Colonial Republics.
[C] Appointment of members of Parliament; dismissal of ministers; dissolution of Parliament; collective ministerial responsibility; and the Dominions.
[D] Appointment of members of Parliament; dismissal of ministers; dissolution of Parliament; collective ministerial responsibility; and the European Union.

16. Which one of the following correctly describes the modern application of the rule of law?

[A] Legality, inequality before the law and institutional morality.
[B] Illegality, inequality before the law and institutional morality.
[C] Legal uncertainty, equality before the law and no subjection to discretionary powers.
[D] Legal certainty, equality before the law and no subjection to discretionary powers.

17. Writing in the 19th century Dicey gave the rule of law three meanings. Which of the following is INCORRECTLY attributed to Dicey?

[A] The absolute supremacy or predominance of regular law.
[B] The law as administered by the ordinary law courts equally for all people.
[C] The jurisdiction of the courts to apply judicial review to legislation.
[D] Constitutional law is not the source but the consequence of the rights of individuals as defined and enforced by the courts.

18. Consider the following immunities often enjoyed by elected representatives:

(i) Freedom from arrest in civil matters.
(ii) Freedom from arrest in criminal matters.
(iii) Freedom from being declared bankrupt.
(iv) Freedom of speech.

Which of the above are the personal privileges of members of Parliament?

[A] The statements in (i) and (ii).
[B] The statements in (ii) and (iii).
[C] The statements in (ii) and (iv).
[D] The statements in (i) and (iv).

19. Which of the following is NOT an example of the right of Parliament to control its internal proceedings?

[A] The right to determine disputed Parliamentary elections.
[B] The right of qualification to sit in the House.
[C] The right to declare a Parliamentary seat vacant.
[D] The right to expel a member of Parliament.

20. In his classical exposition of the 'English Constitution' Walter Bagehot divided Britain's political institutions into the 'efficient' and the 'dignified' parts of the constitution. Which, according to Bagehot, were identified as the 'dignified' parts?

[A] The House of Commons and the House of Lords.
[B] The cabinet and the monarchy.
[C] The House of Lords and the monarchy.
[D] The cabinet and the House of Commons.

21. Who described Britain's constitutional arrangements as a 'disguised republic'?

[A] Walter Bagehot.
[B] Albert Venn Dicey.
[C] Sir Ivor Jennings.
[D] Tony Benn.

22. Writing in the 1970s Lord Hailsham described Britain's system of government as an 'elective dictatorship'. What did he mean by an 'elective dictatorship'?

[A] A politically motivated and unaccountantable judiciary.
[B] A politically motivated and unaccountable civil service.
[C] The absolute legislative power vested in Parliament controlled by a government with a Parliamentary majority.
[D] The delaying powers of the House of Lords.

23. Consider the following fundamental articles of English constitutional law:

(i) That the pretended power of suspending of laws or the execution of laws by regal authority without consent of Parliament is illegal.
(ii) That the levying of money for or to the use of the crown by pretence of the prerogative without grant of Parliament . . . is illegal.
(iii) That the raising or keeping of a standing army within the kingdom in time of peace unless it be with the consent of Parliament is against the law . . .

Where are these provisions, all of which remain in force, to be found?

[A] Magna Carta 1215.
[B] The Petition of Right 1628.
[C] The Bill of Rights 1689.
[D] The Act of Settlement 1700.

24. Under the traditional doctrine of the separation of powers as advocated by Locke in the 17th century and later applied by the French jurist Montesquieu, it was considered desirable for the purposes of maintaining democratic government that the legislative, executive and judicial functions of government should be performed by separate institutions and personnel. Which of the following offices of state requires the holder to participate in all three institutions of state?

[A] The Prime Minister.
[B] The Attorney General.
[C] The Master of the Rolls.
[D] The Lord Chancellor.

25. The pressure group 'Constitution Watch' is concerned that during the third reading of the Compulsory Purchase Bill 1995 (fictitious), all four MPs present in the Common's chamber were drunk and incapable of debating the issues. The Bill subsequently received the Royal Assent and is now the Compulsory Purchase Act 1995. 'Constitution Watch' wish to challenge the validity of the legislation on the grounds of procedural irregularity and fraud during its passage through Parliament. Consider the following:

[A] The courts have jurisdiction to challenge the validity of the legislation on the ground of procedural irregularity.
[B] The courts have jurisdiction to challenge the validity of the legislation on the ground that it was passed fraudulently.
[C] The courts have no jurisdiction to challenge the manner in which the Act was passed.
[D] The court has jurisdiction to disapply those provisions of the Act which are interpreted to be contrary to natural justice.

Which is correct?

26. Which Act of Parliament incorporates and gives effect to European Community law in the United Kingdom?

[A] The Single European Act 1986.
[B] The Treaty on European Union 1992.
[C] The European Communities Act 1972.
[D] The European Communities (Amendment) Act 1986.

27. Which of the following institutions is NOT an institution of the European Union?

[A] The Council of Europe.
[B] The European Council.
[C] The Council of Ministers.
[D] The European Commission.

28. What is the significance of the terms 'monism' and 'dualism' in constitutional law?

[A] The terms describe the relationship between domestic courts and the European Court of Justice.
[B] The terms describe the procedure by which international law acquires legal effect in domestic law.
[C] The terms describe the relationship between domestic law and the law of the European Communities.
[D] The terms describe the relationship between the legal systems of the constituent parts of the UK.

29. Which of the following sources of European Community law automatically becomes part of domestic law without the need for direct or indirect domestic legislation?

[A] The Treaty of Rome 1957.
[B] Regulations.
[C] Directives.
[D] Decisions.

30. The UK Parliament has recently passed the British Apples Preference Quota Act 1995 (fictitious) which requires all shops in the United Kingdom to offer for sale 85% of apples of British origin. Whilst the Act remains silent on this point, it conflicts with the provisions of European Regulation 94/999 which provides that no member-state's domestic law may discriminate on grounds of nationality when offering apples for sale. How will the British courts approach this apparent conflict between domestic and Community legislation?

[A] The 1995 Act is an expression of Parliamentary sovereignty (supremacy) and must therefore prevail.
[B] The 1995 Act must prevail, being the later legislative enactment to be preferentially applied under the normal rules of statutory interpretation.
[C] The 1995 Act must be disapplied in favour of Regulation 94/999 in recognition of the inherent supremacy of Community law.
[D] The English courts must refer the matter to the European Court of Justice under the preliminary rulings jurisdiction of Article 177.

31. The UK Parliament has recently passed the British Apples Preference Quota Act 1995 (fictitious) which requires all shops in the UK to offer for sale 85% of apples of British origin. The Act expressly repeals the provisions of European Regulation 94/999 which provides that no member-state's domestic law may discriminate on grounds of nationality when offering apples for sale. How will the British courts approach this apparent conflict between domestic and Community legislation?

[A] The 1995 Act is an expression of Parliamentary sovereignty (supremacy) and must therefore prevail.
[B] The 1995 Act must prevail; litigants can sue the British government for damages under the *Francovich* principle (see *Francovich v Italy* (cases C-6 & 9/90, (1992) IRLR 84).
[C] The 1995 Act must be disapplied in favour of Regulation 94/999 in recognition of the inherent supremacy of Community law.
[D] The English courts must refer the matter to the European Court of Justice under the preliminary rulings jurisdiction of Article 177.

32. Which Code of Practice attached to the Police and Criminal Evidence Act 1984 deals with statutory police powers to stop and search?

[A] Code A.
[B] Code B.
[C] Code C.
[D] Code D.

33. PC Dilligent who is about to go out on uniformed foot patrol is asking your advice about the requirements for a lawful search under s. 1 of the Police and Criminal Evidence Act 1984 and the Code of Practice. Which of the following guidance points written in his notebook is INCORRECT?

[A] The suspect must be in a public place or a place to which the public have access.
[B] The officer can stop and search for 'stolen or prohibited' articles.
[C] To be acting lawfully, the officer having stopped a suspect under s. 1 must always search for 'stolen or prohibited articles'.
[D] The officer must comply with the Code of Practice.

34. The lawful exercise of powers to stop and search under s. 1 of the Police and Criminal Evidence Act 1984 is dependent on the officer having 'reasonable suspicion' that the suspect is in possession of 'stolen or prohibited articles'. Consider the following statements.

(i)   Reasonable suspicion is determined by the circumstances of each case and is objectively assessed.
(ii) Reasonable suspicion can be determined by the suspects age, hairstyle and manner of dress.
(iii) Reasonable suspicion is determined by the suspect's previous convictions for the possession of stolen or prohibited articles.
(iv) Reasonable suspicion is determined by the information the officer has received and the time and place that powers under s. 1 are exercised.

Which of the above statements can the police officer lawfully take into account when determining the existence of 'reasonable suspicion'?

[A]   The statements in (i) and (ii).
[B]   The statements in (i) and (iii).
[C]   The statements in (ii) and (iv).
[D]   The statements in (i) and (iv).

35. Charlie was about to smash the side window of a Ford Escort when he was apprehended by PC Dilligent. Dilligent said to Charlie: 'Its a fair cop son. You'd better come with me.' Charlie was taken to the police station where he arrived at 5 p.m. He was seen by the custody officer who left him alone in an interview room until 5.32 p.m. when PC Dilligent informed him that he'd been arrested on suspicion of attempting to take a motor vehicle without the owner's consent. Charlie was then cautioned. Consider the legality of Charlie's arrest.

[A] The arrest is unlawful as Charlie wasn't told the grounds of the arrest at the first reasonable opportunity as required by the Police and Criminal Evidence Act 1984 (PACE).
[B] The arrest is lawful as Charlie is a well-known car thief and knows all about police powers.
[C] The arrest is unlawful until Charlie is informed of the reason for his detention by PC Dilligent at the police station.
[D] The arrest is lawful as it was obvious why Charlie was arrested and therefore it was not necessary under PACE for Charlie to be told the grounds of his arrest.

36. Emma is driving her sports car at 125 mph along the M25 when she is stopped by PC Anxious. She admits that she was speeding, promises to drive more carefully and provides full documentation to confirm her identity. Emma is shocked to hear PC Anxious tell her that she is under arrest for speeding and that she should accompany him to the police station. Is the arrest lawful?

[A] The arrest is lawful because speeding is an arrestable offence as defined by s. 24 of the Police and Criminal Evidence Act 1984 (PACE) and can be made without a warrant.
[B] The arrest is lawful because speeding is a non-arrestable offence under s. 25 of PACE and can be made without a warrant.
[C] The arrest is lawful because speeding is a non-arrestable offence under s. 25 of PACE and one or more of the arrest conditions applies which allows the arrest to be made without a warrant.
[D] The arrest is not lawful because speeding is non-arrestable offence under s. 25 of PACE and none of the arrest conditions apply which allows the arrest to be made without a warrant.

37. Nick has been arrested and detained at the police station on suspicion of having committed a series of burglaries. The investigating officer DC Slimey has been called away on another case. In order to save time and as a favour to DC Slimey, the custody officer Sergeant Right has offered to interview Nick. Is this permitted under the provisions of PACE?

[A] Yes, provided the custody officer has the investigating officer's permission.
[B] Yes, where the purpose is to speed up the investigation.
[C] No, the custody officer is required to remain impartial from the investigation.
[D] No, unless Nick consents to the interview.

38. Which of the following is NOT an intimate sample for the purposes of PACE?

[A] Saliva and swabs from the mouth.
[B] Urine.
[C] Dental Impression.
[D] Blood.

39. Which of the following is NOT advocated as a legitimate reason for the UK enacting a formal, written, constitutional document?

[A] Its necessary to limit the legislative omnipotence of Parliament.
[B] Its a requirement of the UK's obligations under the Treaty on European Union (1992) (the Maastricht Treaty).
[C] Its desirable to make the country's constitutional arrangements more intelligible and accessible.
[D] It would provide an opportunity for a complete review of the UK's constitutional arrangements.

40. Consider the following statements of the changes made by the passing of the Public Order Act 1986. Which is INCORRECT?

[A] The Act abolished certain common law public order offences.
[B] The Act created completely new statutory public order offences.
[C] The Act restated the common law public order offences in statutory form only.
[D] The Act created administrative procedures for the control of public order.

41. Louise is the organiser of the Broomhead Witches' March which has been held in the Broomhead village every May Day since 1311. Mrs Busybody has advised Louise that under s. 11 of the Public Order Act 1986 she is required to give notice to the police about the annual procession. Louise seeks your advice. Which of the following is correct?

[A] For the purposes of s. 11 of the Public Order Act 1986 the Broomhead Witches' March does not constitute a 'procession' and notice is not required.
[B] The Broomhead Witches' March comes within the ambit of s. 11 and notice is required.
[C] The Broomhead Witches' March takes place on the village green and therefore is not covered by s. 11 which covers processions on the public highway only.
[D] The Broomhead Witches' March is likely to be excluded from the notice provisions of s. 11.

42. Which of the following is NOT specifically a reason for the police imposing conditions on a public procession under s. 12 of the Public Order Act 1986?

[A] Serious injury to the public.
[B] Serious public disorder.
[C] Serious damage to property.
[D] Serious disruption to the life of the community.

43. For the purposes of the definition of what constitutes a 'public assembly' under s. 16 of the Public Order Act 1986, what is the minimum number of people that must be present?

- **[A]** 10.
- **[B]** 20.
- **[C]** 50.
- **[D]** 75.

44. For the purposes of the definition of 'riot' under s. 1 of the Public Order Act 1986, what is the minimum number of people that must be present?

- **[A]** 3.
- **[B]** 10.
- **[C]** 12.
- **[D]** 20.

45. Both offences of 'riot' under s. 1 and 'violent disorder' under s. 2 of the Public Order Act 1986 require, for the prosecution to prove each offence, that 'a person of reasonable firmness . . . fears for his personal safety'. Consider the following statements about the test to be employed in determining the meaning of 'a person of reasonable firmness':

(i) The person of 'reasonable firmness' has to be present at the scene of the offence.
(ii) The person of 'reasonable firmness' does not have to be present at the scene of the offence.
(iii) The effect of the defendant's actions on an unusually frail or nervous witness can be taken into account.
(iv) The effect of the defendant's actions on an unusually frail or nervous witness cannot be taken into account.

Which statements apply the correct test?

- **[A]** The statements in (i) and (ii).
- **[B]** The statements in (i) and (iii).
- **[C]** The statements in (ii) and (iv).
- **[D]** The statements in (iii) and (iv).

46. Which of the following statements correctly identifies how s. 4 of the Public Order Act 1986 (the offence of 'threatening behaviour') can be committed?

[A] Threatening, violent, insulting words or behaviour.
[B] Intimidating, violent, insulting words or behaviour.
[C] Threatening, violent, abusive words or behaviour.
[C] Threatening, abusive, insulting words or behaviour.

47. Which notoriously controversial section of the Official Secrets Act 1911 was used to prosecute in *R v Ponting* [1985] Crim LR 318 and was subsequently repealed by the Official Secrets Act 1989?

[A] Section 1.
[B] Section 2.
[C] Section 5.
[D] Section 10.

48. Which of the following statements correctly identifies the Official Secrets Acts currently in operation?

[A] The Official Secrets Acts 1911, 1920, 1989.
[B] The Official Secrets Acts 1920, 1956, 1989.
[C] The Official Secrets Acts 1911, 1956, 1989.
[D] The Official Secrets Acts 1911, 1920, 1956.

49. Which of the following two statements correctly identifies the categories of information covered by the Official Secrets Act 1989, ss. 1–4?

(i) Information relating to security, intelligence and defence.
(ii) Information beneficial to an enemy of the state.
(iii) Information relating to international relations and criminal investigations.
(iv) Information prejudicial to the interests of the state and national security.

[A] The statements in (i) and (ii).
[B] The statements in (ii) and (iii).
[C] The statements in (iii) and (iv).
[D] The statements in (i) and (iii).

50. Section 12 of the Official Secrets Act 1989 defined the category of persons who could commit an offence under ss. 1–4. Which of the following occupations is NOT caught by these provisions?

[A] An MP.
[B] An administrative assistant in the Department of Social Security.
[C] A police officer.
[D] A lorry driver, employed by a private company, delivering plastic bags to government offices.

51. Consider the following statements about potential defences to prosecutions under ss. 1–4 of the Official Secrets Act 1989.

(i) The disclosure of the information was in the public interest.
(ii) The information disclosed had already been published.
(iii) The defendant believed she had lawful authority to disclose the information.
(iv) The defendant reasonably believed the information disclosed was not one of the restricted categories in ss. 1–4.

Which of the above 2 statements correctly identifies the defences available?

[A] The statements in (i) and (ii).
[B] The statements in (i) and (iii).
[C] The statements in (ii) and (iv).
[D] The statements in (iii) and (iv).

52. The devolution of governmental powers has long been a possible solution to bringing government 'closer' to the constituent parts of the UK. Which of the following statements correctly defines in constitutional terms, what is meant by the term 'devolution'?

[A] The constitutional allocation of power and responsibilities between national and regional governments on the basis of equality.
[B] The delegation of central government powers leaving overriding control in the hands of Parliament.
[C] Central government only performing those tasks which cannot be performed more effectively at a local or regional level.
[D] The irrevocable withdrawal of functions from central to local or regional government.

53. By which name is the British electoral system popularly known?

[A] The single transferable vote system.
[B] The additional member system.
[C] The party list system.
[D] The first past the post system.

54. Free elections are an essential characteristic of a popular majoritarian democracy like the UK. On how many occasions however since 1945 has a government been elected after receiving more than 50% of the total votes cast nationally?

[A] No government has been elected with more than 50% of the votes cast.
[B] Two governments have been elected with more than 50% of the votes cast.
[C] Five governments have been elected with more than 50% of the votes cast.
[D] Seven governments have been elected with more than 50% of the votes cast.

55. Which of the following leading legal and political figures has NOT at some time supported the UK adopting a formal written constitutional document?

[A] Tony Benn.
[B] Lord Hailsham.
[C] Margaret Thatcher.
[D] Lord Scarman.

56. Which of the following is NOT included in the accepted constitutional meaning of the 'Crown'.

[A] The executive.
[B] The state.
[C] The administration.
[D] The government.

57. Which office of State also assumes the role of 'First Lord of the Treasury'?

[A] The Chancellor of the Exchequer.
[B] The financial secretary to the Treasury.
[C] The speaker of the House of Commons.
[D] The Prime Minister.

58. The pressure group Save Every Tree (SET) is seeking a declaration from the High Court that a decision by the Ministry of Agriculture to allow 120 acres of prime forest to be felled and released for industrial development is unlawful. The empowering legislation, The Tree Felling Regulations 1989 (fictitious), states that the 'decision to allow the development of forest areas shall be made by the minister'. Save Every Tree have discovered on this occasion that the decision was made by a civil servant. Advise SET on the legality of the decision.

[A] The decision is lawful as the minister is entitled to delegate such powers to civil servants.
[B] The decision is unlawful as the civil servant has acted *ultra vires*.
[C] The decision is unlawful as the Parliament expressly requires the decision to be made by the minister.
[D] The decision is unlawful as the minister should have delegated the decision-making powers to another minister.

59. Which of the following is NOT part of Parliament's scrutiny of the executive?

[A] The Select Committees.
[B] The Public Accounts Committee.
[C] The Comptroller and Auditor General.
[D] The 1922 Committee.

60. Parliament is seeking to establish a Bill of Rights. You are asked to advise which of the following forms of entrenchment is INCOMPATIBLE with traditional principles of constitutional theory.

[A] Repeal or amendment of the Bill of Rights can only be achieved after a unanimous vote of the House of Commons.
[B] Repeal or amendment of the Bill of Rights can only be achieved with the consent of the majority of the people.
[C] Protection from amendment or repeal of the Bill of Rights will be achieved by the incorporation of a 'notwithstanding clause'.
[D] Protection from amendment or repeal of the Bill of Rights will be achieved by inserting a clause that the 'present and all future Parliaments will abide by the content and spirit of the Bill'.

MCT2

[TIME LIMIT : $2\frac{1}{2}$ HOURS]

ADMINISTRATIVE LAW

1. Consider the following statements:

(i) Administrative law enables the tasks of government to be carried out.
(ii) Administrative law governs the legal relationship between the administrative agencies of the State.
(iii) Administrative law governs the legal relationship between the administrative agencies of the State and the public.
(iv) Administrative law provides some of the ways in which the administrative agencies of the State are held accountable for the exercise of powers under statute and the prerogative.

Which of the above statements correctly identifies the scope and purposes of modern administrative law?

[A] The statements in (i) and (ii).
[B] The statements in (ii) and (iii).
[C] The statements in (i), (ii) and (iv).
[D] All the statements.

2. Which one of the following institutions of government is NOT subject to control by administrative law?

[A] Parliament.
[B] Government ministers.
[C] Civil servants.
[D] Local authorities.

3. Which court exercises the 'inherent supervisory' jurisdiction in administrative law?

[A] The Crown Court.
[B] The Queens Bench Division of the High Court.
[C] The Chancery Division of the High Court.
[D] The County Court.

4. Consider which ONE of the following statements correctly identifies the theories which provide the constitutional foundations of administrative law.

[A] The theories of the rule of law, Parliamentary sovereignty and the separation of powers.
[B] The theories of Parliamentary sovereignty, entrenchment and the separation of powers.
[C] The theories of entrenchment, the separation of powers and the rule of law.
[D] All of the theories.

5. The French system of administrative law (the Droit Administratif) differs from the English system in a number of ways. Consider the following characteristics attributed to the Droit Administratif:

(i) A separate system of administrative courts and tribunals dealing exclusively with administrative law.
(ii) A jurisdiction which imposes special duties, privileges and immunities upon the State's administrative bodies.
(iii) A jurisdiction based in case law and precedent.
(iv) The Conseil D'Etat being the model for the European Court of Justice.

Which of the above statements correctly identifies the characteristics of the Droit Administratif?

[A] All of the statements.
[B] The statements in (i), (ii) and (iii).
[C] The statements in (i), (iii) and (iv).
[D] The statements in (ii), (iii) and (iv).

6. Harlow and Rawlings in *Law and the Administration* (1984), suggest that theorists writing about the aims and purposes of administrative law can be categorised into 'red-light', 'green-light' or 'amber-light theorists'. Which one of the following statements correctly describes the amber-light theorists?

[A] The purpose of administrative law is to uphold individual liberties against enchroachment by public bodies.
[B] The purpose of administrative law is to uphold individual liberties against encroachment by public bodies and to facilitate the implementation of government policies.
[C] The purpose of administrative law is to facilitate the implementation of government policies.
[D] The purpose of administrative law is to facilitate the implementation of European Community law.

7. As a matter of policy, for the purposes of judicial review proceedings, are all statutory and prerogative powers exercised by public bodies, justiciable?

(i) As a matter of policy all statutory powers are justiciable.
(ii) As a matter of policy the exercise of some statutory powers are non-justiciable.
(iii) As a matter of policy all prerogative powers are justiciable.
(iv) As a matter of policy the exercise of some prerogative powers are non-justiciable.

Which two of the above statements is correct?

[A] The statements in (ii) and (iv).
[B] The statements in (i) and (iii).
[C] The statements in (i) and (iv).
[D] The statements in (ii) and (iii).

8. Consider the following statements about the court's purpose when exercising its inherent jurisdiction in judicial review proceedings:

(i) The court has the power to review the case and substitute its own decision for that of the public body.
(ii) The court is only concerned with the way in which the public body has applied its statutory or common-law powers.
(iii) The court does not substitute its decision for that of the public body but directs the public body to apply their powers lawfully.
(iv) The court conducts a full rehearing of both the relevant law and facts of the case.

Which statements correctly identify the purpose of judicial review proceedings?

[A] The statements in (i) and (ii).
[B] The statements in (ii) and (iii).
[C] The statements in (iii) and (iv).
[D] The statements in (ii) and (iv).

9. Is judicial review inconsistent with the traditional theory of the legislative supremacy of Parliament?

[A] Yes, because judicial review enables judges to question the validity of an Act of Parliament.
[B] Yes, because judicial review enables unelected judges to undermine the democratic principles of Parliament.
[C] No, because judicial review as a matter of policy is only concerned to ensure proper administration by public bodies, tribunals and inferior courts and is not concerned with matters of political significance.
[D] No, because judicial review ensures the will of Parliament is carried out by administrative bodies, tribunals and inferior courts.

10. Lord Diplock's speech in *O'Reilly* v *Mackman* [1983] 2 AC 237 provides the basis of the modern law of where judicial review proceedings under RSC O. 53 are intended to apply. (The 'exclusivity principle'.) Which 1 of the following reasons did Lord Diplock NOT refer to in support of the exclusivity principle?

[A] The time limits in judicial review proceedings prevent the decisions of public bodies being questioned at an unreasonably late stage.
[B] The procedural requirements of judicial review provide safeguards against public bodies being the victims of vexatious litigation.
[C] It was inappropriate for public law bodies to have civil law remedies ordered against them.
[D] The procedural inadequacies of the judicial review prior to 1977 had been remedied by the 'new' procedure.

11. In *O'Reilly* v *Mackman* [1983] 2 AC 237, Lord Diplock recognised that there would be exceptions to the 'exclusivity rule'. Which 1 of the following situations would NOT provide an adequate reason for public law issues to be decided by an action commenced by writ or originating summons?

[A] Where the issue of public law arises by way of a defence.
[B] Where the public law issue is a collateral matter.
[C] Where none of the parties object to the adoption of a procedure commenced by writ or originating summons.
[D] Where one of the parties to the action wanted to claim damages.

12. One of the consequences of the decision in *O'Reilly* v *Mackman* [1983] 2 AC 237 is that judicial review is available only against a respondent which is defined as a 'public body'. The Court of Appeal in *R* v *Panel on Take-overs and Mergers, ex parte Datafin plc* [1987] 1 All ER 564, provided guidelines as to what constitutes a public body. Which one of the following would the court NOT consider to be a factor which makes an organisation susceptible to judicial review?

[A] The source of the body's power is under the common law.
[B] The body is created or empowered by statute.
[C] The body takes decisions which affect the public.
[D] The body's constitution provides for appeal against its rulings.

13. Applying the principles laid down by the Court of Appeal in *R v Panel on Take-overs and Mergers, ex parte Datafin plc* [1987] 1 All ER 564, which 1 of the following organisations has been held to be a 'public body' and therefore susceptible to judicial review?

[A] A City Technical College.
[B] National Greyhound Racing Club Ltd.
[C] A fee paying school.
[D] The Jockey Club.

14. You are the legal adviser to the pressure group Save Every Tree (SET) which is seeking judicial review of the Secretary of State's decision to destroy 120 acres of prime forest in Northumberland to make way for a new theme park. When deciding the issue of the group's *locus standi* to challenge the decision, which of the following factors will the court NOT find in the group's favour?

[A] SET is an influential pressure group in environmental matters and has 130 members in the vicinity of the proposed theme park.
[B] SET is seeking an order for *mandamus*.
[C] SET is alleging a substantial and serious breach of statutory powers by the Secretary of State.
[D] SET is the only group with the expertise and interest to challenge the decision.

15. Andrew wishes to seek judicial review against the decision of Sodsbury Council not to allow him planning permission. He wants to initiate proceedings immediately. Which one of the following is the most accurate advice to give him about applying for judicial review?

[A] Show no sufficient interest in standing; apply within 3 months; case must not be vexatious or frivolous; and issue a writ in the High Court.
[B] Show *locus standi*; apply within 3 months; case must be vexatious or frivolous; and file an application and affidavit with the High Court.
[C] Show *locus standi*; apply within 3 months; case must not be vexatious or frivolous; and file an application and affidavit with the High Court.
[D] Show *locus standi*; apply within 2 months; case must not be vexatious or frivolous; and file an application and affidavit with the County Court.

16. The House of Lords in *Council of Civil Service Unions* v *Minister for the Civil Service* [1985] AC 374 (the *GCHQ* case) established that there were three grounds for judicial review. One of the following statements accurately reflects their Lordships' findings. Which one?

[A] Illegality, irrationality and procedural impropriety.
[B] Illegality, unreasonableness and procedural impropriety.
[C] Illegality, irrationality and procedural fairness.
[D] Illegality, irrationality and natural justice.

17. Which one of the following statements INCORRECTLY defines the boundaries of irrationality as a substantive ground in judicial review proceedings?

[A] Where the decision maker has failed to follow the correct procedure.
[B] Where the decision maker imposes onerous conditions to a decision.
[C] Where the decision maker has failed to have regard to those factors which were legally relevant.
[D] Where a decision is so unreasonable no reasonable authority could ever have come to it.

18. Section 5 of the Dismissal of the Public Servants Regulations 1995 (fictitious) requires that before public servants can be lawfully dismissed, on the grounds of misconduct: 'they shall have their case put before the Public Servants Disciplinary Tribunal'. Barry, a public servant who is currently the subject of disciplinary hearings, is seeking judicial review of the tribunal's decision not to allow him an oral hearing at which he wished to be legally represented. The tribunal has decided that it will consider written representations only. Advise Barry which one of the following principles the court is likely to apply when giving its judgment.

[A] The word 'shall' is not a mandatory requirement and provides the Disciplinary Tribunal with complete discretion was to how disciplinary matters are dealt with.
[B] Barry is entitled to an oral hearing but not legal representation.
[C] Barry is entitled to an oral hearing and legal representation.
[D] Barry is entitled to make representations to the tribunal but is not entitled to an oral hearing or legal representation.

19. The Minister for Land Use has been given powers by Parliament under s. 2 of the Land Use (Amenities) Act 1996 (fictitious) to 'manage the land in its possession or control in the best interests of the state'. Exercising powers under s. 2, the minister has banned stag hunting on land controlled by the Department of Land Use, because she considers stag hunting to be immoral. The Stag Hunting Society is seeking judicial review of the decision. Which one of the following approaches is the court likely to adopt?

[A] The minister's actions are lawful because Parliament has given the Minister wide discretion.
[B] The minister is entitled to take into account moral considerations when exercising the statutory powers.
[C] The minister will have to show how the moral considerations are relevant to the exercise of the statutory powers.
[D] The minister is not entitled to take into account moral considerations.

20. You represent Carlos, a convicted Colombian drug dealer. On 3 June, Carlos was told in a letter from the Home Secretary that he would be deported under s. 5A of the Drug Offenders Deportation Act 1995 (fictitious) which allows him the right of appeal against the Home Secretary's decision to deport him. On 5 June, Carlos received another letter from the Home Secretary which informed him that he was to be deported under s. 5B of the Drug Offenders Deportation Act 1995 which provides no right of appeal against the Home Secretary's decision. Carlos will be deported in 6 days time. To what extent can Carlos rely on the doctrine of legitimate expectation when he seeks judicial review of the Home Secretary's decision to use his powers under s. 5B?

[A] The Home Secretary's letter of 3 June gives rise to the legitimate expectation that the deportation would be ordered under s. 5A.
[B] The doctrine of legitimate expectation will only apply where Carlos can show that it is unfair or detrimental to good administration for the Home Secretary to depart from his initial decision.
[C] The doctrine only applies to those decisions where the applicant is entitled to be consulted and consultation has not taken place as required.
[D] The doctrine of legitimate expectation has no application as Carlos doesn't enjoy any existing rights or benefits which are affected by the Home Secretary's decision.

21. Anytown District Council has established a voluntary scheme with Anytown Insurance Company by which the council's tenants pay an additional £2 per week for their household insurance. The sum is included in the weekly rent, is to be collected by the council and administered by the Anytown Insurance Company. The council believes it is permitted to do this by s. 34 of the Council Housing Act 1989 (fictitious) which provides that the 'general management, regulation and control' of council houses is vested in the local authority. A rival insurance company, Besteverquote, believes the scheme is unlawful. Advise Besteverquote.

[A] The scheme is *intra vires* the council's powers as it is reasonably incidental to those expressly conferred.
[B] The scheme is *ultra vires* the council's powers as it falls outside the powers expressly conferred.
[C] The scheme is illegal as it is 'unreasonable' for local authorities to be involved in the collection of insurance premiums for insurance companies.
[D] The scheme is unlawful as it has fettered the council's discretion.

22. The Anytown District Council is given statutory powers to determine planning applications 'according to the recognised powers and procedures allowed by law'. Anytown is the first local authority to introduce a scheme whereby all applicants for planning permission have to pay a £20 preliminary fee for each planning application. Betterquality Builders plc are lodging with Anytown District Council an application to build 500 executive-style homes. Advise Betterquality Builders which one of the following grounds the court is likely to apply when determining the legality of the preliminary fee scheme in judicial review proceedings.

[A] The scheme is *intra vires* as it is incidental to the statutory powers already conferred.
[B] The scheme is *intra vires* as the statutory powers confer local authorities with a wide discretion as to how they discharge their functions.
[C] The charge is unlawful as it is 'unreasonable'.
[D] The scheme is *ultra vires* as no charge can be levied on the public without clear statutory authority.

23. Parliament has recently passed the Student Loans Recovery Act 1995 (fictitious) which provides powers that 'the Department of Education should recover £250 from all students who received student grants between 1991 and 1993'. Sue is seeking judicial review against the decision of the Department of Education to demand repayment of the £250 by July 1996. Which one of the following principles is the court likely to apply?

[A] The Department's decision is *ultra vires* and unlawful.
[B] The effect of the Act is retrospective and will not be applied as it is contrary to the rules of natural justice.
[C] The Department's decision is 'unreasonable' and therefore will not be applied.
[D] The Department's decision is *intra vires* and lawful.

24. Erika has been found guilty of driving without due care and attention at Anytown Magistrates' Court. Erika has discovered that the clerk who sat with the magistrates is the sister of another driver involved in the accident for which Erika has just been found guilty. Although the clerk played no part in the court's decision to find her guilty, Erika is unhappy about her sitting. Advise Erika which one of the following principles of natural justice is likely to be applied to her case.

[A] The conviction will stand unless Erika can show there was actual bias.
[B] The principle of judicial independence requires that the rules of natural justice have no application to the magistrates' court.
[C] The conviction will stand as none of the magistrates had a personal interest in the case.
[D] The conviction will be overturned as the appearance of bias is enough to offend the rules of natural justice.

25. You represent Barry and Sarah who have been 'administratively discharged' from the Navy on the grounds of their homosexuality. They seek judicial review of the decision. Consider which one of the following grounds the court is likely to apply when making its decision.

[A] The decision is rational having been approved by both Houses of Parliament.
[B] The decision is irrational.
[C] The decision is unlawful as it contravenes the European Convention on Human Rights.
[D] The decision is non-justiciable as it is an exercise of prerogative power.

26. There has been a trend in recent judicial decisions to require that administrative bodies should be required to give reasons for their decisions. (For example, see *Doody* v *Home Secretary* [1993] 3 All ER 92.) Which one of the following statements therefore correctly identifies the present position?

[A] There is a general requirement that all public bodies are required to give reasons for their decisions.
[B] Whilst there is no general requirement there are classes of cases where public bodies have a duty to give reasons for their decisions.
[C] There is no recognised requirement in English law for public bodies to give reasons for their decisions.
[D] There is a requirement but only where the issue raised a question of European Community law where the duty to give reasons is a recognised ground for judicial review.

27. It has been suggested that ever since Coke, Holt and Mansfield laid the foundations for judicial review the legislature has attempted to prevent those principles being built upon. Which one of the following is NOT an ouster clause in legislation which seeks to exclude the judicial review jurisdiction of the courts?

[A] A 'finality' clause.
[B] A 'time limits' clause.
[C] A 'conclusive evidence' clause.
[D] An 'as if enacted' clause.

28. The decision of the House of Lords in *Anisminic v Foreign Compensation Board* [1969] 2 AC 147 is one of the most important decisions in modern administrative law. Which one of the following principles did the decision in *Anisminic* establish?

[A] Powers exercised under royal prerogative were justiciable.
[B] Only errors of law within the jurisdiction of the public body were reviewable.
[C] All errors of law outside the jurisdiction of the public body were reviewable.
[D] Judicial review could lie against a public body irrespective of whether it was exercising a judicial or administrative function.

29. Where does the duty of individual civil servants lie?

[A] To Parliament.
[B] To the cabinet.
[C] To the public.
[D] To the minister of the Crown in charge of the civil servant's department.

30. One of the criticisms made against the office of the Parliamentary Commissioner for Administration (PCA) is traditionally the low level of public awareness about its role and responsibilities. In 1994 how many complaints were referred to the PCA?

[A] 1,322.
[B] 590.
[C] 230.
[D] 140.

31. Which of the following is INCORRECTLY ascribed to the office of the Parliamentary Commissioner for Administration (PCA)?

[A] The PCA receives written complaints from the public which have been filtered through a constituency member of Parliament.
[B] The PCA can investigate allegations of maladministration in only those government departments listed in sch. 2 of the Parliamentary Commissioner Act 1967.
[C] Even where a matter falls within the jurisdiction as defined by sch. 2, the PCA has discretion whether to accept the complaint.
[D] Where the PCA accepts jurisdiction and investigates the complaint the PCA has power to grant a remedy and compensation where 'maladministration' has been proven.

32. Susan seeks your advice about obtaining judicial review against the Parliamentary Commissioner for Administration (PCA) in respect of a complaint she made to her member of Parliament (MP) about the actions of the Department of Social Security. What advice would you give to Susan?

[A] As a matter of policy the commissioner's decisions are non-justiciable.
[B] As a servant of Parliament, redress against a decision of the commissioner lies exclusively through Susan's MP.
[C] The court's power to review the commissioner's actions lies only in those exceptional cases where there was 'abuse of discretion'.
[D] The commissioner's role and statutory framework makes his decisions susceptible to judicial review.

33. The meaning of 'maladministration' is not defined by the Parliamentary Commissioner Act 1967 but is found in the so-called Crossman catalogue. Which of the following characteristics of decision making by subordinate bodies is NOT cited in the Crossman catalogue?

[A] Bias, neglect, inattention.
[B] Delay, incompetence, ineptitude.
[C] Wilful, illogical, unreasonable.
[D] Perversity, turpitude, arbitrariness.

34. The extension of the office of an 'ombudsman' into new areas of responsibility is a recent trend in the development of administrative accountability. Which of the following ombudsmen does NOT hold office?

[A] The Parliamentary Commissioner for Standards.
[B] The Legal Services Commissioner.
[C] The European Community ombudsman.
[D] The Citizen's Charter ombudsman.

35. Into which category of administrative accountability does the Parliamentary Commissioner for Administration fit?

[A] Legal.
[B] Quasi-legal.
[C] Political.
[D] None of these.

36. Which of the following correctly identifies the constitutional relationship between central and local government?

[A] Local government exercises its functions under a devolved system with central government.
[B] Local government exercises its functions under a federal system with central government.
[C] Local government exercises its functions under a policy of subsidiarity with central government.
[D] Local government exercises its functions as a quasi-governmental body.

37. There have been numerous reports and inquiries into the structure and functions of local government. One of the most celebrated, the Widdicombe Committee (The Conduct of Local Authority Business 1986), identified three positive benefits deriving from the British system of local government. Which one of the following is INCORRECTLY ascribed to the Widdicombe Committee?

[A] Responsiveness, in that it contributes to the provision of local needs through the delivery of services.
[B] Accountability, in that it provides an effective check on the exercise of powers by central government.
[C] Participation, in that it contributes to local democracy.
[D] Pluralism, in that it contributes to the national political system.

38. In order to fulfil their administrative functions local authorities have to exercise *intra vires* their legal powers. Which one of the following statements correctly identifies the source of these powers?

[A] Powers conferred by the common law and Parliament.
[B] Powers conferred by the European Community and the common law.
[C] Powers conferred by custom and Parliament.
[D] Powers conferred by Parliament and the European Community.

39. Consider the following statements about the functions of local government:

(i) The raising of finance through taxation.
(ii) Planning control.
(iii) A law-making function.
(iv) A licensing and regulatory function.

Which one of the following correctly identifies the extent of local government's statutory powers and responsibilities?

[A] The statements in (i) and (iii).
[B] The statements in (i), (ii) and (iii).
[C] The statements in (ii), (iii) and (iv).
[D] All of them.

40. Which of the following is NOT a recognised structure of local government?

[A] Metropolitan County Council.
[B] Metropolitan Borough Council.
[C] Unitary Council.
[D] Non-Metropolitan District Council.

41. Parliament's delegation of law-making powers to subordinate public bodies is justified for a number reasons. Which of the following is NOT an acceptable reason for passing delegated legislation?

[A] It relieves pressure on Parliament's valuable time.
[B] It enables technical legislation to be passed which couldn't be the subject of meaningful debate in Parliament.
[C] It is the practical manifestation of the view that Parliament is no longer legislatively sovereign.
[D] It provides for flexibility in the legislative process.

42. The delegation of legislative powers applies to a wide range of government business. It is suggested that some legislative enactments should not be in delegated form. Which one of the following is recognised as an acceptable purpose for passing delegated legislation?

[A] Where the delegated powers incorporate European Community law.
[B] Where the delegated powers enact matters of general principle.
[C] Where the delegated powers sub-delegate legislative authority to another body.
[D] Where the delegated powers have retrospective operation.

43. Which one of the following types of subordinate legislation is NOT subject to the Statutory Instruments Act 1946?

[A] Statutory Orders in Council.
[B] Immigration Rules under the Immigration Act 1971.
[C] Rules of the Supreme Court.
[D] Town planning development orders.

44. Judicial review enables the courts to control the exercise of powers under delegated legislation. Which one of the following statements INCORRECTLY describes the court's jurisdiction to review the exercise of delegated legislative powers?

[A] As a matter of policy, delegated legislation deals only with 'justiciable' issues.
[B] The jurisdiction of the courts to review the exercise of delegated powers can never be excluded by the parent Act.
[C] Under the doctrine of Parliamentary sovereignty the validity of primary legislation cannot be questioned by the courts.
[D] Delegated legislation will never provide the subordinate body with absolute substantive and/or procedural powers.

45. When reviewing the legality of the exercise of delegated powers by subordinate bodies, which of the following sources of law has a presumptive status only?

[A] European Community law.
[B] The parent Act.
[C] The European Convention on Human Rights.
[D] The common-law principles of 'natural justice'.

46. The Joint Select Committee on Statutory Instruments is required to scrutinise all statutory instruments, whether laid before Parliament or not. Which of the following is NOT a reason for the Committee to make a report to Parliament?

[A] It is intended that the instrument should operate retrospectively.
[B] The parent Act excludes review by the courts.
[C] The instrument imposes a tax.
[D] The instrument gives effect to Community law.

47. Which of the following public bodies or offices does NOT possess the legislative authority to make delegated legislation?

[A] Judges.
[B] The universities.
[C] The Nature Conservancy Council.
[D] Local authorities.

48. One of the consequences of the growth of the modern state in the 20th century has been the dramatic rise in the use of delegated legislative powers. Approximately, how many statutory instruments were passed in 1995?

[A] 740.
[B] 3,000.
[C] 8,000.
[D] 15,000.

49. What kind of function did the Franks Report 1957 identify as being exercised by most statutory tribunals?

[A] Adjudicatory.
[B] Administrative.
[C] Review.
[D] Supervisory.

50. The complex system of statutory tribunals is an inevitable manifestation of the modern administrative state. Which one of the following would NOT be cited as a justifiable reason for establishing a system of tribunals?

[A] Tribunals encourage greater procedural informality and public accessibility.
[B] Tribunals provide greater control over powers of appointment and tenure.
[C] Tribunals encourage greater expertise and specialist knowledge by the decision-makers.
[D] Tribunals are more suitable for the implementation of social policy than the courts.

51. In view of the wider purposes of administrative law, advise the Minister of State for Administrative Affairs, which one of the following forms of accountability, is the LEAST suitable to determine disputes between the individual and the newly created Welfare Benefits Agency (fictitious).

[A] A Welfare Benefits Appeal Tribunal.
[B] The County Court.
[C] The Welfare Benefits Agency.
[D] The Welfare Benefits Ombudsman.

52. Consider the following statements about tribunals in administrative law.

(i) The procedure in tribunals is inquisitorial.
(ii) Tribunals have a limited jurisdiction.
(iii) Errors of law are subject to judicial review.
(iv) The procedure in tribunals is adversarial.

Which of the following answers correctly identifies the essential characteristics of tribunals?

[A] The statements in (i), (ii) and (iii).
[B] The statements in (ii), (iii) and (iv).
[C] The statements in (i) and (ii).
[D] The statements in (ii) and (iii).

53. Some (not all) tribunals are classified as 'inferior' courts, within the terms of RSC O. 52, r. 1(2)(iii), and are therefore subject to the law of contempt. Which one of the following characteristics, applied to the nature of a tribunal's jurisdiction, is NOT indicative of the status of being an 'inferior' court.

[A] The tribunal determines disputes between individuals and the State.
[B] The tribunal decides cases affecting the rights of the parties.
[C] The tribunal can administer the oath.
[D] The tribunal can compel the attendance of witnesses.

54. Which of the following is or are a source of procedural rules for the conduct of public inquiries?

[A] Each of the sources listed below.
[B] Section 9 of the Tribunals and Inquiries Act 1992.
[C] The rules of natural justice.
[D] The Council on Tribunals.

55. You represent Edmund who is seeking injunctive relief against the Minister of Administrative Affairs after his failure to recognise an order of the High Court. Which one of the following statements correctly identifies the legal position?

[A] Injunctions can be issued against ministers of the Crown.
[B] Parliamentary privilege excludes the jurisdiction of the court to grant injunctive relief against ministers.
[C] The Crown Proceedings Act 1947 grants immunities to ministers preventing injunctive relief being granted against them.
[D] Injunctive relief will not be granted as ministers are servants of the Crown and enjoy the same immunities as the Crown.

56. Sonia is a civil servant who works in the Department of Administrative Supplies. In contravention of the Department's regulations, Sonia contracts with 'Bestvalu Teabags Ltd' for the supply of 15,000 teabags. (The regulations, allow her to contract for the supply of 10,000 teabags only.) 'Bestvalu' deliver the 15,000 teabags as required and are now told that the Department of Administrative Supplies are refusing to pay. Advise Bestvalu of their legal position in relation to the breach of contract.

[A] The court will not enforce the contract as the Department can claim Crown immunity from being sued in the courts.
[B] The court will not enforce the contract and therefore Bestvalu should proceed against the Crown under the Petition of Right Act 1860.
[C] The Crown is liable to fulfil its obligations under the contract.
[D] As Sonia was acting outside her authority the Crown are not liable and can invoke the defence of 'executive necessity'.

57. It has been suggested that as a fundamental principle of administrative fairness, public bodies should be bound by their decisions or statements which affect private persons. Which one of the following statements correctly identifies the doctrine of estoppel as applied by *Western Fish Products Ltd* v *Penwith DC* [1981] 2 All ER 204 to public authorities?

[A] The decision established that the doctrine of estoppel has no application to public authorities.
[B] The decision established that the doctrine of estoppel applies to all decisions and statements made by public authorities.
[C] The decision established that the doctrine of legitimate expectation and not estoppel as the most appropriate form of redress.
[D] The doctrine of estoppel applies to a limited range of statements and decisions.

58. After 12 years of service, Raymond has been dismissed from his post in the Department of Administrative Affairs. As the alleged reason for his dismissal was 'misconduct' Raymond was not even allowed to serve his period of notice. As a former Crown servant he seeks your advice about the legal remedies open to him to pursue financial compensation against his former employers. Which one of the following correctly identifies the legal remedies available to former Crown employees?

[A] An action for unfair dismissal at an industrial tribunal.
[B] An action for wrongful dismissal in the County Court.
[C] Both [A] and [B].
[D] Neither [A] nor [B].

59. Which case forms the basis of the modern law of public interest immunity?

[A] *Compagnie Financiere et Commerciale Du Pacifique* v *The Peruvian Guano Co.* (1883) 11 QBD 55.
[B] *Duncan* v *Cammell Laird & Co.* [1942] AC 624.
[C] *Ellis* v *Home Office* [1953] 2 QB 135.
[D] *Conway* v *Rimmer* [1968] AC 910.

60. Which one of following statements correctly identifies the scope of public interest immunity (PII)?

[A] PII applies only to civil proceedings.
[B] PII applies only criminal proceedings.
[C] The same principles of PII apply to both civil and criminal proceedings.
[D] PII applies to both civil and criminal proceedings but is subject to distinctive approaches.

APPENDIX 1

ANSWERS TO MCT1

1. C	16. D	31. A	46. D
2. B	17. C	32. A	47. B
3. A	18. D	33. C	48. A
4. B	19. A	34. D	49. B
5. C	20. C	35. C	50. A
6. A	21. A	36. D	51. D
7. C	22. C	37. C	52. B
8. C	23. C	38. A	53. D
9. B	24. D	39. B	54. A
10. A	25. C	40. C	55. C
11. C	26. C	41. D	56. B
12. B	27. A	42. A	57. D
13. D	28. B	43. B	58. A
14. C	29. B	44. C	59. D
15. A	30. C	45. C	60. D

APPENDIX 2
ANSWERS TO MCT2

1. D
2. A
3. B
4. A
5. A
6. B
7. A
8. B
9. D
10. C
11. D
12. D
13. A
14. B
15. C

16. A
17. A
18. D
19. C
20. B
21. A
22. D
23. D
24. D
25. A
26. B
27. B
28. C
29. D
30. A

31. D
32. D
33. C
34. D
35. C
36. A
37. B
38. D
39. D
40. A
41. A
42. A
43. B
44. B
45. C

46. D
47. B
48. B
49. A
50. B
51. C
52. B
53. A
54. A
55. A
56. C
57. D
58. A
59. D
60. D

APPENDIX 3

NOTE-FORM ANSWERS TO MCT1

1. An easy question to begin but one which raises a fundamental issue – what is a constitution? Answer [C] is correct. Confusingly writers interchangeably use the word in both its narrow and wide meanings. The statement in (i) (the narrow meaning) comes from Wade and Bradley *Constitutional and Administrative Law*, (ed. Bradley and Ewing), 11th edn, Longman, 1993. It applies to those legal systems with a formal constitutional document, having special legal status which sets out the functions of the governmental institutions, their relationship with each other and with the people. Accompanying the document will be a Supreme or Constitutional Court which has jurisdiction to question the validity of governmental actions where they are considered 'unconstitutional'. The USA and Germany have this system. The statement in (ii) reflects the wider meaning of 'constitution' and is taken from Hood, Phillips and Jackson *Constitutional and Administrative Law*, 7th edn, Sweet & Maxwell, 1987. Whilst not contained in a single formal document, the constitution relates to the collection of the laws and non-legal rules upon which government operates. Britain's constitutional arrangements come within this wider definition.

2. Again a simple question but a topic which students often find confusing. Answer [A] is incorrect. All political and legal systems need rules through which to operate. Answer [D] is incorrect and relates to those constitutional provisions which can only be amended or repealed if special legislative procedures are followed. Answer [C] is always popular but is also wrong. Most of Britain's 'constitutional' law is in written form including Acts of Parliament, judicial decisions and European Community law. Unlike many legal systems the law and non-legal rules are not contained in a single document known as the 'constitution' but come from a variety of sources. For this reason [B] is correct. Much of the British constitution is in written form but has not been codified.

3. Apart from the basic characteristic of a constitution being written or unwritten, there are various other characteristics which can be applied. Answer [B] is correct – the British constitution is bicameral in that it establishes two legislatures: the House of Commons and the House of Lords. Answer [C] is also correct. The British state is unitary in that whilst there is more than one tier of government, legislative authority is based on a hierarchical order. The British government, through Parliament, controls the other tiers of government – see the discontinuance of the Northern Ireland Parliament in 1972. Answers [A] and [D] come from Bryce (1901) vol. 1 Essay 111, in which he described the procedures for amending constitutions. Answer [D] relates to those constitutions where no special procedures are required to invoke constitutional change. This characteristic is correctly applied to Britain's flexible constitution. Answer [A] relates to those constitutions which require a special procedure before amendments to the constitution can be made, for example through a national referendum. This is incorrectly applied to Britain and is the answer you should have chosen. For further discussion see Thompson, *Introduction to Constitutional and Administrative Law*.

4. Answer [A] is incorrect. In a well-established line of authorities the court's constitutional role has clearly been stated to interpret and give effect to the will of Parliament. The courts are under a similar constitutional duty in respect of European Community law, answer [D], since the European Communities Act 1972, s. 2(4) and judicially confirmed by the decision in *Factortame No. 2* [1991] AC 603. The courts will also recognise and give effect to prerogative powers [C]. Since the landmark House of Lords' decision in *Council of Civil Service Unions v Minister of State for the Civil Service* [1985] AC 374 and confirmed in *R v Secretary of State for Foreign and Commonwealth Affairs, ex parte Everett* [1989] QB 811 the courts will review the way in which some prerogative powers are exercised. [B] is the correct answer although to what extent the courts refuse to recognise and give effect to conventions is unclear. Dicey's proposition that conventions are never recognised and enforced by the courts is probably wrong. In some areas where conventions operate, for example, ministerial responsibility, the courts may recognise the convention: see *Liversedge* v *Anderson* [1942] AC 206. It is probably true to say, however, that whilst Dicey's contention is generally correct it is not without exceptions.

5. The question is a good example of Sir Ivor Jenning's view that conventions 'provide the flesh which clothes the dry bones of the law'. Answer [A] is incorrect because statements (i) and (iii) establish the legal position of the monarch in these matters. In law the monarch still has the right to withhold the royal assent from legislation and has a complete discretion as to who should be appointed as Prime Minister. However, accepted constitutional practice, justified through the doctrine of the 'limited monarchy', requires that royal assent should always be given to a validly enacted Bill and that the leader of the largest party in the House of Commons should be invited to form 'Her Majesty's government'. Answer [C] is therefore correct.

6. The question concerns the status of prerogative powers and their relationship with statute law. Answer [D] is incorrect. Since the decision in *Council of Civil Service Unions* v *Minister of State for the Civil Service* [1985] AC 374 the exercise of prerogative powers are potentially justiciable. Answers [B] and [C] are incorrect because the courts will not recognise the prerogative being exercised in a particular manner where Parliament has intervened: see *Attorney General* v *de Keyser's Royal Hotel* [1920] AC 508. Answer [A] is correct. The minister's actions are unlawful: see *R* v *Secretary of State for the Home Department, ex parte Fire Brigades Union* [1995] 2 WLR 1. The prerogative cannot be used to introduce the radically different compensation tariff.

7. Dicey's view of 'parliamentary sovereignty' is the most enduring statement in British constitutional theory. In the *Law of the Constitution*, Dicey expressed the view that legally 'the sovereignty of Parliament was the dominant characteristic of our political institutions'. It had three characteristics: answer [A] the Queen in Parliament has the right to make or unmake any law; answer [D] no person or body recognised by British law has the right to override or set aside Parliamentary legislation; and answer [B] that political sovereignty resides with the electorate, whose views are represented by members of Parliament which have a limiting effect on Parliament's seemingly unchallengeable legal powers. The correct answer is [C]. The quotation is attributed to Blackstone, *Commentaries*, pp. 160, 161, upon whose original theory of the sovereignty of Parliament, Dicey based much of his work.

8. Revisionists of Dicey's theory have come to recognise that constitutional and political developments have placed potential limitations on the legislative supremacy of Parliament. It has been suggested that [A] the Act of Union with Scotland created a new Parliament which did not inherit the unlimited authority of the English Parliament. For judicial support of this view see the comments of Lord Cooper in *MacCormick* v *Lord Advocate* 1953 SC 396. By s. 4 of the Statute of Westminster answer [B] Parliament appears to be voluntarily limiting its legal authority to legislate in the former Dominions. For a practical example see Viscount Radcliffe's *dicta* in *Ibralebbe* v *R* [1964] AC 900. Answer [C] is obviously incorrect. The European Communities Act 1972 provides the most potent limitation on the legislative authority of Parliament. Community law is not only part of British law but is inherently superior and must be applied when in conflict with domestic law. Some Community law (regulations) automatically become part of British law without the legislative sanction of Parliament. Answer [C] is correct. The European Convention of Human Rights is not incorporated into British law by an Act of Parliament and therefore whilst Britain may be breaching its obligations in international law, the courts would be required to apply domestic legislation in conflict with the Convention.

9. Answer [D] is wrong. Section 24(7) of the Police and Criminal Evidence Act 1984 does provide wider powers of arrest but can only be lawfully exercised by police officers. Answer [A] is also incorrect. Even where Lucy can show 'reasonable grounds' *R* v *Self* [1992] 3 All ER 476 is authority to suggest that she can only lawfully detain where an arrestable offence has been committed. David's acquittal proves no offence was committed and no power of arrest existed. A similar rationale can be applied to answer [C]. The correct answer is therefore [B].

10. Part IV of the Police and Criminal Evidence Act 1984 and Code C of the Codes of Practice deal with the detention of suspects at police stations. In determining when Alex needs to be released the period of lawful detention runs from the 'relevant time' – his arrival at the police station. Answers [C] and [D] under s. 43 require warrants of further detention from the magistrates' court. These have not been obtained and are incorrect. Answer [B] is dealt with by s. 42 and requires an authorisation of continued detention by a senior police officer. For s. 42 to apply Alex needs to be charged with a serious arrestable offence as defined by s. 116(6)(f). It is unlikely the offence for which Alex has been arrested comes within the subsection: see *R v McIvor* [1987] Crim LR 409 and *R v Smith* [1987] Crim LR 579. Therefore [B] is wrong and [A] is correct. Alex is required to be released after 24 hours: s. 41.

11. Answer [B] accurately establishes that a 'threat' for the purposes of s. 3 cannot be constituted by words alone: s. 3(3) of the Public Order Act 1986. Answer [A] also accurately establishes that David ordering the dog to attack was sufficient to constitute a 'threat' under s. 3: see *R v Dixon* [1993] Crim LR 579. Answer [C] is the correct answer. The test for 'conduct causing fear' is accurately laid down in [D].

12. The law as to what amounts to the 'State's interest' is to be found in *Chandler v DPP* [1964] AC 763. Their Lordships specifically excluded the Crown [A], the government [C] and the subjective view of the defendant [D]. The correct answer is the test laid down in answer [B] – the 'State's interest' as defined by the organised community at large (*per* Lord Reid at p. 790).

13. Blackstone suggested that freedom of expression consists 'in laying no previous restraints upon publication' (*Blackstone's Commentaries on the Laws of England*, 16th edn, London, 1825 p. 151). However, unlike the USA, English law uses both prior and subsequent legal, quasi-legal and administrative provisions to limit freedom of expression. Answer [A] is an administrative provision of prior restraint – classifying films and videos before they go on general release. Answer [B] is also an example of prior restraint and invariably applying an interim injunction to prevent publication of the offending material: see *Argyll v Duchess of Argyll* [1967] Ch 302 and *Attorney-General v Guardian Newspapers (No. 2)* [1990] 1 AC 109. Answer [C] is also incorrect. Ignoring a 'D' notice, whilst having no legal status, could lead to a newspaper being prosecuted under the Official Secret Acts. The 'D' Notice Committee gives advice as to whether sensitive information should be published in newspaper articles and is a limitation of prior restraint. [D] is the correct answer. An action in defamation is an example of limiting freedom of expression through subsequent restraint.

14. The non-legal rules of the UK's constitutional arrangements are described by Dicey as 'Conventions'. These he describes as 'understandings, habits, practices, customs, maxims and precepts': see Dicey, A. V., *An Introduction to the Study of the Law of the Constitution*, London: MacMillan, 1959, pp. 24 and 417. Also, see Thompson, *Textbook on Constitutional and Administrative Law*, London: Blackstone Press, 2nd edn. 1995, Ch. 4, p. 64. These non-legal rules are unenforceable in law, as evidenced by the Privy Council's ruling in *Madzimbamuto v Lardner-Burke* [1969] 1 AC 645. Even so, conventions can regulate the Crown's discretionary powers due to innate obedience surrounding these rules for fear that without such compliance, political and legal difficulties might prevail. Although Jennings disagrees with Dicey's analysis if this obedience, Dicey's presumption explains the wide-usage of the right to resign by ministers.

15. Examples of UK constitutional conventions are best categorised into four sections: sovereign–Parliament relations; executive–Parliament relations; Parliamentary conventions; and the Commonwealth. The sovereign–Parliament relations includes the appointment of Prime Minister, dismissal of ministers and the dissolution of Parliament, which may, in law, amount to an exercise of the sovereign's personal prerogatives, but which in practice, are closely controlled by conventions. Incidents of ministers and cabinet exercising individual and collective ministerial responsibilities clearly demonstrate the importance of conventions. The best example being the Westland Affair in 1985. The day-to-day administration of Parliament is governed by many wide-ranging Parliamentary conventions. For instance, voting divisions in the House of Commons; by-election rules; the judicial work of the House of Lords; and the relationship between the two Houses of Parliament. The Commonwealth poses a curious example following the Balfour Declaration in 1926 and the subsequent Statute of Westminster 1931. Yet where some of the former colonies and new Dominions retain the monarch as Head of State or in her capacity as Head of the Commonwealth, the conventions of sovereign consultation and royal assents remain. The only notable exceptions are the Republics of India and South Africa, Canada (Canada Act 1982) and Australia (Australia Act 1986).

16. Professor Jowell's advice that the 'Rule of Law has meant many things to many people' (Jowell & Oliver, *The Changing Constitution*, 3rd edn, Oxford: Oxford University Press, 1994, Ch. 3, p. 57) is well known to students of constitutional law. As a constitutional principle, the doctrine of the rule of law is often confused with the separation of powers or the doctrine of responsible government upon which it relies. Students should look to Dicey for an accepted, authoritative definition who wrote that:

> Law is the result of the judicial decisions determining the rights of private persons in particular cases brought before the courts . . . Every official, from the Prime Minister down to a constable or a collector of taxes, is under the same responsibility for every act done without legal justification as any other citizen . . . No one is punishable or can lawfully be made to suffer in body or goods except for a distinct breach of the law before the ordinary courts of the land (Dicey, *Law of the Constitution*, 1885, 1959 in Wade, E. C. S. (ed.) pp. 195, 193 and 188)

The quotation provides us with three meanings – certainty of law, equality before the law and no subjection to arbitrary or discretionary powers. The rule of law therefore is a principle of institutional morality which maintains certainty and procedural fairness within our constitutional framework. The cases of *Prohibitions del Roy* (1607) 12 Co Rep 63 and *Entick* v *Carrington* (1765) 19 St Tr 1030 support Dicey's classical view. Answer [D] is therefore correct and answers [A], [B] and [C] incorrect.

17. All students of constitutional law are required to understand Dicey's interpretation of the meaning of Parliamentary sovereignty and the rule of law. In the *Introduction to the Study of the Constitution*, Dicey gave three meanings to the rule of law. Answer [A] correctly identifies the first meaning of the 'absolute supremacy or predominance of the regular law'. Answer [B] identifies the second meaning; 'equality (of all) before the law'. Answer [D] is the third reason that constitutional law is not 'the source but the consequence of the rights of individuals'. Answer [C] is therefore incorrectly attributed to Dicey's classical interpretation of the rule of law.

18. If members of Parliament are to work effectively they are required to enjoy certain immunities known as 'Parliamentary privileges'. There are two types of privilege: the collective privileges of the House and the personal privileges of individual members. This question is concerned with the privileges of individual members, of which there are two. The first is freedom from arrest in civil matters for a period of 40 days before to 40 days after a session of Parliament. Since the abolition of imprisonment for civil debt this has symbolic rather than practical significance. The immunity does not extend to criminal proceedings nor does it prevent a member from being declared bankrupt. The most important privilege remains freedom of speech. A member is immune from any criminal or civil suit for what he has said or done in Parliament. Answer [D] is therefore the answer which correctly identifies the personal privileges of members of Parliament.

19. The collective privileges of the House of Commons enables Parliament to perform its constitutional functions more effectively and to be free from outside interference either from the courts or directly by the executive. Answer [B] correctly identifies the right of Parliament to decide whether a member is qualified to sit in the House. Answer [C] correctly identifies the privilege to declare a seat vacant and answer [D] the right to expel a member. Answer [A] incorrectly identifies a privilege which is no longer exercised by Parliament but determined by statute. Answer [A] is therefore the answer required.

20. Along with Dicey, Walter Bagehot is the most celebrated of constitutional writers. First published in book form in 1867 the English Constitution classically describes the golden age of Parliamentary government, which after the passing of the Reform Act also in 1867, rapidly declined. Despite the speed with which the accuracy of his observations were overtaken by political events, Bagehot provided a unique insight into government and the distribution of power. He divided the country's constitutional institutions into the 'dignified' and 'efficient' parts. The dignified parts he identified as the House of Lords and the monarchy. Answer [C] is correct. The efficient parts, where political power was really exercised were the House of Commons and the cabinet as suggested in answers [A], [B] and [D] which are incorrect.

21. In his analysis of the distribution of political power in late 19th century Britain, Walter Bagehot observed that the monarchy had lost many of its former powers to the institutions of popular government, the House of Commons and the cabinet. Whilst the monarchy retained important symbolic functions, as the exercise of real constitutional powers lay elsewhere, government could correctly be described as a 'disguised republic'. Answer [A] is therefore correct and answers [B], [C] and [D] incorrect.

22. The term 'elective dictatorship' was first coined by Lord Hailsham in October 1976 during his Dimbleby Lecture, a theme he returned to later in his book the *Dilemma of Democracy* (1978). The term described the potential threat posed by a government with a Parliamentary majority which might, by using the absolute legislative power vested in Parliament, introduce legislation which threatened the fundamental principles of the UK's democratic traditions. The phrase accurately reflects the concentration of political power in the hands of the executive and the lack of effective channels of accountability to keep the executive in check. As a counterweight to these potential abuses of power Lord Hailsham advocated a written constitution and a Bill of Rights. Answer [C] is therefore correct and answers [A], [B] and [D] incorrect.

23. It is important to recognise, in the absence of a formal written constitutional document, where the sources of the UK's constitutional law are to be found. Legislation is the most important source and the enactments cited in this question have over the centuries established many fundamental constitutional principles which remain relevant today. Answer [A], the Magna Carta, formally recognised the rights of the people against arbitrary and capricious treatment in the administration of justice and taxation. Answer [B], the Petition of Right, identified the injustice of the king imposing taxation without Parliamentary consent and arbitrary imprisonment. Answer [D], the Act of Settlement, provided for succession to the throne and added important provisions to the Bill of Rights from which the citations in the question are taken. Answer [C] is therefore the correct answer.

24. The logic of the doctrine of the separation of powers is that it guards against the concentration of power in too few hands, making government more democratic and accountable. In the UK the doctrine is not strictly adhered to. By convention, in recognition of ministerial responsibility to Parliament, government ministers (the executive) are required also to be members of the legislature (the House of Commons or the Lords). As a general rule the judiciary is independent of both Parliament and the executive. Therefore answer [A], the Prime Minister, is a member of two institutions of state only, as is the Attorney General, answer [B], the government's chief legal officer. Answer [C], the office of the Master of the Rolls, is a member of the judiciary only. Answer [D] is correct. The Lord Chancellor sits in all three institutions of state. The holder of the office is head of the judiciary, a member of the executive and the *ex officio* speaker of the House of Lords.

25. Unlike many legal systems, British courts do not have the inherent right to review the constitutionality of legislation or the way in which it proceeded through the legislative process. Since the Glorious Revolution of 1688 and the establishment of Parliamentary supremacy, the constitutional role of the courts has been to give effect to and apply the will of Parliament. Answers [A] and [B] are therefore incorrect. Answer [D] may have had some validity in the dim and distant past. Chief Justice Coke in *Dr Bonham's Case* (1610) 8 Co Rep 114 spoke of the common law having the power to control Acts of Parliament and judge them 'utterly void'. That clearly is not however the position today. Answer [C] is correct, supported by a line of authority including *Ex parte Canon Selwyn* (1872) 36 JP 54, *Pickin v British Railways Board* [1974] AC 765 and *Manuel v Attorney General* [1983] Ch 77.

26. The United Kingdom adopts a dualist approach to the incorporation of international treaty obligations into domestic law. This means that an Act of Parliament is necessary before the provisions of the treaty will be recognised and enforced by the domestic courts and tribunals. Therefore the signing of the European Community treaties without further Parliamentary action would have had no effect in English law. Answer [C], the European Communities Act 1972, was passed to give effect to Community law in the UK and is the correct answer. Sections 2 and 3 of this vitally important piece of legislation should be familiar to all students of constitutional law.

Answer [A], the Single European Act 1986, is incorrect because it is not an Act of Parliament but a European Treaty which put into force many of the economic objectives of the Community such as free movement of capital, goods and services. Answer [D] is incorrect as this is the Act of Parliament which incorporated the provisions of the Single European Act. Answer [B] is also incorrect. The Treaty on European Union, the Maastricht Treaty, has been ratified by Parliament but not incorporated into English law.

27. To facilitate the attainment of its political, economic and legal objectives, the European Community and Union has developed a sophisticated institutional structure. Answer [B] is correctly identified as a Union institution. Since 1974 it has been the formal title given to the twice yearly meeting of the heads of governments and foreign ministers. The Council of Ministers is also correctly identified. The Council has legislative and executive powers and defends the national interests of the Member States. Answer [D], the Commission, is also an institution of the Union. It is the administrative arm of the organisation and has been described as the engine which drives the Community forward. The Council of Europe, answer [A], is not an institution of the Union and is the correct answer. The Council is the organisation which oversees the European Convention on Human Rights.

28. The terms 'monism' and 'dualism' describe the way in which a state recognises and incorporates international law into their domestic legal systems. Answer [B] is the correct answer. The UK is a dualist state. Primary or delegated legislation is required before international law creates rights and obligations that are recognised and enforced by the English courts. For a practical illustration, compare the status of European Community law and the European Convention on Human Rights 1950. A monist state, such as France, automatically incorporates international law into domestic law on the signing or ratification of the treaty. Answers [A], [C] and [D] are incorrect.

29. European Community law can be divided into primary or secondary sources. Answer [A], the Treaty of Rome 1957, is the most important of the primary sources and lays down the fundamental objectives of the European Community and Union. As the UK is a dualist state, for the provisions of the Treaty to have effect in domestic law, it was necessary for Parliament to pass the European Community Act 1972. Answer [A] is therefore incorrect. Answer [C] refers to Directives which, whilst being an important secondary source, do not automatically have legal effect in the domestic jurisdiction of a Member State. Answer [D], Decisions, are addressed to States and/or individuals and do not automatically take effect. Answer [B] is therefore correct. The provisions of Regulations are binding on Member States in their entirety and are directly applicable requiring no legislative implementation.

30. The relationship between the inherent superiority of European Community law (see *Van Gend en Loos* v *Nederlandse Administratie der Belastingen* case 26/62 [1963] ECR 1, *Costa* v *ENEL* case 6/64 [1964] ECR 585 and numerous other authorities) and the traditional theory of Parliamentary supremacy has been the most perplexing issue in modern constitutional law. The incorporation of Community law into the UK is provided for by ss. 2 and 3 of the European Communities Act 1972. Section 2(4) requires that '. . . any enactment passed or to be passed . . . shall be construed and have effect subject to the foregoing provisions of this section'. The effect of ss. 2 and 3 appears to limit the sovereign power of Parliament to legislate on any subject. United Kingdom legislation must be construed to comply with Community law. This was position set out by the House of Lords in *R* v *Secretary of State for Transport, ex parte Factortame Ltd (No. 2)* [1991] 1 AC 603. Therefore answers [A] and [B] which reflect the traditional position of Parliamentary supremacy are incorrect. Answer [D] is also incorrect. A reference under Article 177 is concerned with a question of interpretation of Community law and not national law. Answer [C] therefore correctly interpets the provision of the European Communities Act 1972 and the decision in *Factortame*.

31. Observant students will recognise that in this question the Act of Parliament expressly repeals the provisions of the Community Regulation. It would appear therefore that the traditional view of Parliamentary supremacy will prevail. Applying *Macarthys Ltd* v *Smith* [1979] ICR 785, answer [A] is correct.

32. There are five Codes of Practice attached to the substantive provisions of the Police and Criminal Evidence Act 1984. It is a specific requirement that they should be available at all police stations to be consulted by police officers, people detained by the police and members of the public. The Codes do not have the status of the substantive law but rather are suggested guidelines for the police to follow when exercising their investigative powers. Breaches of the Code have strong evidential implications for the court to take into account when deciding if the police have acted lawfully. Code A deals with statutory police powers to stop and search and therefore answer [A] is correct. Answer [B] is incorrect as Code B deals with police powers to search premises, answers [C] and [D] are also incorrect as those Codes deal with the detention and questioning of suspects and the identification of suspects, respectively.

33. Before 1984 there was no general police power to stop and search, although some forces such as the Metropolitan Police in London did possess some local powers. Section 1 of the Police and Criminal Evidence Act 1984 provides all police officers with the lawful powers to stop and search provided the following criteria are met. Answer [A] correctly identifies the powers must be exercised in a 'public place or a place to which the public have access' s. 1(1). Answer [D] correctly identifies that the officer must comply with Code A, which requires the officer to identify himself, the object of the search and the grounds for making it. Answer [B] recognises that s. 1 powers can be used in relation to stolen or prohibited articles which are defined by s. 1(8A). Answer [C] is the answer you need. There is no requirement under s. 1, that having stopped a suspect, a search needs to occur.

34. The police officer must have reasonable grounds for suspicion before powers of stop and search under s. 1 of the Police and Criminal Evidence Act 1984 can be lawfully exercised. Whilst 'reasonable suspicion' is not defined in the Act, Code A provides guidance as to the criteria the officer can take into account. There must be an objective basis for their belief applied in the circumstances in which the power is to be exercised; for example, the information the officer has received. Therefore the statements in answer [D] are correct. The officer may never base a suspicion on personal factors alone or on the suspect's previous convictions. The statements in answers [A], [B] and [C] are incorrect.

35. Although the Police and Criminal Evidence Act 1984 remains silent as to what amounts to an arrest, s. 28 has broadly adopted the common-law principles in *Christie* v *Leachinsky* [1947] AC 473. In addition to a police officer having the necessary grounds, in this case under s. 24, for an arrest to be lawful the arrested person must be informed of the fact of the arrest and the grounds of the arrest. Answers [B] and [D] are incorrect. Answer [A] is also incorrect. An arrest which is initially unlawful can be made lawful when the arrested person is told the grounds for the arrest. Answer [C] is correct: see *R* v *Kulynycz* [1971] 1 QB 367 and *Lewis* v *Chief Constable of South Wales* [1991] 1 All ER 206. Applying the decision in Lewis, Charlie will be able to sue the police for wrongful arrest from the moment he was detained to the time the arrest became lawful at 5.32 p.m.

36. Sections 24 and 25 deal with the powers of arrest available under the Police and Criminal Evidence Act 1984. Section 24 allows an arrest to be made without a warrant in respect of an arrestable offence as defined by law. The speeding offence which Emma admits to is not an arrestable offence making answer [A] incorrect. Section 25 allows a police officer to arrest a suspect without a warrant in respect of a non-arrestable offence only where one or more of the general arrest conditions provided by s. 25 apply. Answer [B] is incorrect as it does not refer to one of the arrest conditions required. Answer [C] is also incorrect because none of the arrest conditions under s. 25 appear to apply. Answer [D] is therefore correct as Emma's arrest is unlawful.

37. Part IV of the Police and Criminal Evidence Act 1984 (PACE) and Code C deal with the treatment of suspects detained at the police station. Section 36(5) of PACE requires the custody officer to be independent of the investigation and therefore answer [C] is correct.

38. The important difference between intimate and non-intimate samples under the Police and Criminal Evidence Act 1984 (PACE) is that generally the latter can be taken from the suspect without their consent. Sections 54 and 58 of the Criminal Justice and Public Order Act 1994 amend ss. 62 and 65 of PACE so that saliva and swabs from the mouth are now categorised as non-intimate samples. Answer [A] is therefore correct as answers [B], [C] and [D] all relate to intimate samples.

39. Answer [A] correctly identifies that for many commentators, for example Lord Hailsham writing in 1978 in *Dilemma of Democracy* and the Liberal Democrats, the establishment of a written formal, constitutional document is necessary to limit the legislative omnipotence of Parliament. Answer [C], the educative value of a written constitution, improving the accessibility of information and knowledge about constitutional affairs can assist in the smooth functioning of a representative democracy. Answer [D] is also correct. Tony Benn in his Commonwealth of Britain Bill in 1991 sees the introduction of a written constitution as an opportunity to overhaul and fundamentally change the system of government. Answer [B] is the correct answer, in that whilst the Treaty on European Union may have certain constitutional implications, for example, the establishment of a citizenship of Europe (Article 8 of the EC Treaty), it is not a requirement of the UK's obligations under the Treaty to enact a formal written constitution.

40. The passing of the Public Order Act 1986 (POA) can be seen in part as the government's reaction to the widespread civil disorder which occurred during the late 1970s and 1980s. The inner city riots in 1981, violent industrial disputes culminating in the miner's strike in 1984–85 and the continuing problem of football hooliganism all contributed to a climate of strife which required Parliament to revise and codify public order legislation. Answer [A] correctly identifies that the POA abolished certain common-law offences and put them on a statutory footing. Answer [B] is also correct. Some new statutory offences were created and the provisions of others extended. Answer [D] is correct. The 1986 legislation establishes important administrative procedures, for example, under s. 11, requiring compliance by the organiser of public processions. Answer [C] is therefore incorrect. The 1986 Act did considerably more than put common-law offences in a statutory form.

41. The march will come within the accepted common law meaning of a 'procession' as per *Flockhart* v *Robinson* (1950) 2 KB 498 and answer [A] is wrong. Answer [C] is also wrong. Section 16 refers to processions 'in a public place', to include not only the highway but also places to which the public have access which includes the village green. Answer [D] is correct and answer [B] incorrect. The march is likely to be one of the excluded categories of processions which require notice; see s. 11(2) which provides exemption from the notice requirements for those processions commonly or customarily held in the police area.

42. The power to impose conditions on public processions under s. 12(1) arise where a senior police officer reasonably believes it will result in serious public disorder. Answer [B] is therefore correct. Serious damage to property, answer [C], is correct and serious disruption to the life of the community, answer [D], is correct. Therefore serious injury to the public is not specifically a reason cited by the Public Order Act 1986 and answer [A] applies.

43. The definition of what constitutes a 'public assembly' under the Public Order Act 1986 is provided for by s. 16 as: 'an assembly of 20 or more persons in a public place which is wholly or partly open to the air'. Answer [B] is therefore correct.

44. The offence of riot is defined by s. 1 of the Public Order Act 1986 and is the most serious public order offence. Answer [C] is correct. Section 1 requires '12 or more persons who are present together (to) use or threaten unlawful violence . . .'.

45. An essential element to be proven in cases under s. 1 of the Public Order Act 1986 (POA) 'riot' and s. 2, POA 'violent disorder' is that as a result of the defendant's disorderly conduct some person of 'reasonable firmness . . . feared for their personal safety'. The test is hypothetical. It is applied in the context of the average person who might be present at the scene of the offence. Therefore statement (i) referred to in answers [A] and [B] is incorrect. The prosecution cannot adduce evidence of the effect of the disorderly conduct on a person of unusual frailty which would not have affected a person of reasonable firmness. Therefore statement (iii) is not applicable making answer [D] incorrect and answer [C] correctly stating the test to be applied.

46. Section 4 of the Public Order Act 1986 'Fear or provocation of violence' is committed where a person 'uses threatening, abusive or insulting words or behaviour'. Answer [D] is correct and answers [A], [B] and [C] incorrect.

47. Section 2 of the Official Secrets Act 1911 has been one of the most highly criticised enactments in English law; see the Franks Committee recommendations in 1972 (Report, Cmnd 5104). Section 2 made it an offence to disclose any official information. The very wide ambit of the section meant the information didn't have to relate to any matter which might be a threat to national security. After a number of controversial prosecutions under s. 2, culminating in *R v Ponting* [1985] Crim LR 318 the Official Secrets Act 1989 repealed the discredited section. Answer [B] is therefore correct.

48. The criminal offences to be found in the Official Secrets Acts are the most important restrictions on the disclosure of official and secret information. Three Official Secrets Acts remain in force: the 1911 Act, the 1920 Act and the 1989 Act. Answer [A] is therefore correct.

49. Parliament's purpose in passing the Official Secrets Act 1989 was to repeal the discredited s. 2 of the 1911 Act. The 1989 Act criminalised the unlawful disclosure of more restrictive categories of official information contained in ss. 1–4 than its infamous predecessor. These related to security and intelligence in s. 1, defence in s. 2, international relations in s. 3 and information relating to criminal and special investigation powers in s. 4. Answer [B] is correct.

50. The class of persons included in ss. 1–4 of the Official Secrets Act 1989 is defined by s. 12 as a 'Crown servant' and 'government contractor'. Crown servant is, by s. 12(1), held to include **all** civil servants, answer [B] and police officers answer [C]. Government contractors employed in the provision of goods and services, answer [D], are caught by s. 12(2). Answer [A] is the correct answer.

51. The Official Secrets Act 1989 provides a limited range of potential defences to prosecutions under ss. 1–4. Answer [A] is incorrect. There is no provision in the Act for defences based on the issue of disclosure in the 'public interest' or that the 'information had already been published'. The two defences that may apply are: first, where the defendant believed she had 'lawful authority' to disclose the information and 'had no reasonable cause to believe otherwise', s. 7(4). Secondly where 'the defendant at the time of the alleged offence did not know, or have reasonable cause to believe, that the information, document or article related to security or intelligence . . . or that the disclosure would be damaging'. This defence is repeated in ss. 1(5), 2(3), 3(4), 4(4) and (5). Statements (iii) and (iv) identify the available defences making answer [D] correct and answers [B] and [C] incorrect.

52. Answer [A] is incorrect. In the context of 'devolution' there is no basis of equality between central and regional authorities. Ultimate political and legal sovereignty remains with central government. Answer [A] reflects a federal system as opposed to a devolved one. Answer [C] is also incorrect as it is the definition of subsidiarity from the *Oxford English Dictionary*. Whilst not yet a principle of European Community law it is recognised in Community treaties (see Article 130 of the Treaty of Rome) and is a developing concept on the European Union's political agenda. Answer [D] is incorrect because devolution does not involve the irrevocable withdrawal of functions from central to local government. Answer [B] is the correct answer. It is the definition of devolution from the *Kilbrandon Report* 1973, para. 543.

53. Answer [A] is incorrect. The alternative vote system is used in parts of the UK, for example, in Northern Ireland local elections and European elections and is often advocated as the most appropriate proportional system to replace existing electoral arrangements. Answer [B] is also incorrect. The additional member system is used in Germany and combines the principles of both the first past the post system and proportional representation. Answer [C] is incorrect. The party list system is used in Israel and requires that each political party nominates a list of candidates. The vote for each party is calculated on a national as opposed to a constituency basis. Answer [D] is correct. The first past the post system returns single member constituency MPs who have obtained a simple majority.

54. The first past the post electoral system returns MPs sitting entirely for single member constituencies. The requirement that each should return a simple majority often means the elected MP gains less than 50% of the total votes cast. The same principle applies on a national share of the votes to the winning political party. Answer [A] is correct. Every single party government since 1945 has been elected to government with less than 50% of the total national votes cast. Answers [B], [C] and [D] are incorrect.

55. Answer [A] is incorrect. Tony Benn in his Commonwealth of Britain Bill, 1991, advocated fundamental constitutional change including the establishment of a written constitution. Answer [B] is also incorrect. Lord Hailsham writing in 1978 advocated a written constitution to promote limited government as did Lord Scarman in 1974 making answer [D] also incorrect. Answer [C] is correct. Margaret Thatcher has never formally advocated that the UK should adopt a formal written constitution.

56. Unlike most other systems of government, the concept of the State is not a well developed or understood concept in UK constitutional law. According to Lord Simon of Glaisdale in *Town Investments Ltd v Department of the Environment* [1978] AC 359 the Crown has become a term of art in constitutional law. It has come to be used as a convenient and shorthand way of describing the 'executive' as in answer [A], the administration as in answer [B] or the government as in answer [D]. Answer [B] is therefore correct. The State is not included in the accepted constitutional meaning of the 'Crown'.

57. The office of Prime Minister has evolved over the centuries through political and constitutional expediency. From 1721 to 1742 Robert Walpole headed the government. His official title was First Lord of the Treasury. The modern office of Prime Minister, developed after the advent of the party system, has invariably been combined with the title of First Lord of the Treasury. Answer [D] is therefore correct and answers [A], [B] and [C] are incorrect.

58. The question is concerned with the relationship between ministerial responsibility and the courts. Ministerial responsibility imposes a duty on a minister to account to Parliament for what they are doing and the actions of their department. As a matter of policy the courts are reluctant to intervene in this constitutional relationship. Even where Parliament has delegated power to a specific minister it is constitutionally permissible for the power to be exercised by a civil servant. Answer [A] is correct. In *Carltona Ltd v Minister of Works* [1943] 2 All ER 560 Lord Greene MR stated that '(C)onstitutionally, the decision of such an official, is of course, the decision of the minister. The minister is responsible and must answer to Parliament for anything that his officials have done under his authority'. Answers [B] and [C] are therefore incorrect. Answer [D] is also incorrect: see *Lavender and Son Ltd v Minister of Housing* [1970] 3 All ER 871.

59. Answer [A], the Departmental Select Committee system identifies one of main areas of Parliamentary scrutiny of the executive. The present system, in place since 1979, establishes committees of backbench MPs to shadow the main government departments. Answer [B] is also incorrect. The Public Accounts Committee, established in 1861, has the power to examine whether money has been spent for the purpose intended by Parliament and whether the expenditure has produced 'value for money'. Answer [C] is also incorrect. The Comptroller is an officer of the House of Commons and head of the National Audit Office. His main role is to ensure that government departments and other public bodies have spent money in an efficient and economical way. Answer [D] is the correct answer. The 1922 Committee is not formally part of Parliament's scrutiny of the executive. It is the committee that represents the views of backbench Conservative MPs.

60. The traditional interpretation of Parliamentary supremacy includes the idea that Parliament can legislate on any subject, including amending or repealing the provisions of a Bill of Rights. Which form of entrenchment is the least appropriate to protect the UK's Bill of Rights from legislative interference? Answer [A] would provide some appropriate protection against repeal or amendment. It is a common entrenching provision that a requisite majority needs to be achieved in a country's legislature before constitutional change can occur. Answer [B] would also be an appropriate form of entrenchment. Some constitutions, for example the Republic of Ireland, requires that constitutional change can only be achieved after the holding of a referendum or some other form of popular vote. Answer [C], the insertion of a 'notwithstanding clause' would be the most appropriate form of entrenchment. The clause would provide that if a later Act was inconsistent with the Bill of Rights, it would only be legally effective if it explicitly stated the offending clause(s) would take effect 'notwithstanding' its incompatibility with the Bill of Rights. Answer [D] is therefore the correct answer: offending one of the fundamental principles of constitutional theory that a Parliament cannot bind either itself or future Parliaments as to the form and content of its legislative acts.

APPENDIX 4

NOTE-FORM ANSWERS TO MCT2

1. The wide-ranging scope of administrative law reflects the complex nature of the modern state and its administrative agencies. Answer [D] is correct. Each statement correctly identifies an important role of administrative law. Statement (i) identifies that administrative law through administrative and legal processes, enables the tasks of government to be carried out. Statements (ii) and (iii) recognise that administrative law governs the legal relationship between administrative bodies and between administrative bodies and the public. Statement (iv) recognises that administrative law provides the legal, quasi-legal and political framework by which administrative bodies are held accountable for the exercise of their statutory powers and duties.

2. As question 1 indicated, one of the fundamental purposes of modern administrative law is to ensure that the State's administrative agencies exercise their powers and duties lawfully. Therefore government ministers [B], civil servants [C] and local authorities [D] are directly affected by this task of administrative law. Answer [A] is the correct answer. Rather than holding Parliament accountable, administrative law seeks to ensure that the will of Parliament is carried out by ensuring that public bodies act substantively and procedurally *intra vires* the powers that Parliament has given to them.

3. Unlike many European legal systems, for example in France and Germany, English administrative law is practised in the ordinary courts. The Queen's Bench Division of the High Court exercises the 'inherent supervisory jurisdiction'. Answer [B] is correct and answers [A], [C] and [D] incorrect.

4. The theories of the rule of law, Parliamentary sovereignty and the separation of powers, provide the constitutional foundations upon which administrative law operates. The rule of law seeks to ensure that every act a public body performs is within the confines of law. Administrative law also seeks to ensure, through judicial review, that public bodies exercise their statutory powers, procedurally and substantively, in the way Parliament intended. The separation of powers is reflected in the inherent supervisory jurisdiction of the High Court, exercised by a judiciary independent of the executive, to rule on the legality of the actions of public bodies. The theory of entrenchment has no direct application and therefore answer [A] is correct and answers [B], [C] and [D] incorrect.

5. The characteristics of the Droit Administratif came famously under the scrutiny of Dicey in his *Introduction to the Law of the Constitution* first published in 1885. Dicey's analysis provided a dismissive account of the French system, preferring the common-law principles applied in England. The characteristics of the Droit Administratif have remained constant since Dicey's time. Statement (i) correctly identifies that the French have a separate system of administrative courts and tribunals. Statements (iii) and (iv) are also correct. Statement (ii) is also correct in that whilst the Droit Administratif takes a special view of the context of the State in which public officials operate, the rules confer not only certain immunities on public servants but also special duties. Answer [A] is correct and answers [B], [C] and [D] are incorrect.

6. According to Harlow and Rawlings, red-light theorists (answer [A]) see the main purpose of administrative law as the protection of individual liberties against encroachment by the State. The value of the common law as the focus for the protection of individual liberties is held important. Dicey would fit into this category. Answer [C], green-light theorists, consider the main purpose of administrative law is to facilitate government action. Writers, such as Jennings, approve of administrative law facilitating the development of the 'interventionist', 'corporate' State. Whilst administrative law may implement Community law through Orders-in-Council and statutory instruments, it

was not specifically a purpose of administrative law recognised by Harlow and Jennings. Answer [B], a modern interpretation of the role of administrative law, is therefore the correct answer.

7. In *Council of Civil Service Unions* v *Minister for Civil Service* [1985] AC 374 the House of Lords established that in order to assess the issue of the justiciability of prerogative powers, the courts would not look at the source of the power but the nature of those powers. In principle the exercise of some prerogative powers were justiciable and amenable to judicial review. Those issues under the prerogative that were non-justiciable are matters of 'high policy': the making of treaties; the defence of the realm etc. For further illustrations of the principle see *R* v *Secretary of State for Foreign Affairs and Commonwealth Affairs, ex parte Everett* [1989] QB 811 and *R* v *Secretary of State for the Home Department, ex parte Bentley* [1993] 4 All ER 442. Statement (iv) accurately reflects the legal position in relation to the prerogative. Similar principles apply to statutory powers. It is assumed that where a statute deals with matters, for example, of national security, the exercise of those powers will be non-justiciable; see *Chandler* v *DPP* [1964] AC 763 in relation to s. 1 of the Official Secrets Act 1911. Statement (ii) accurately reflects the law in relation to statutory powers and answer [A] is correct and answers [B], [C] and [D] are incorrect.

8. The purpose of judicial review is reflected in statements (ii) and (iii). The court is not concerned with the public body's decision itself but procedurally and/or substantively has the public body exercised its powers lawfully? Where the court determines the public body has acted unlawfully, the matter is remitted back to the public body for the decision to be made in a lawful way. Statements (i) and (iv) reflect a system of appeal not review. The distinction is important. Answer [B] is correct and answers [A], [C] and [D] are incorrect.

9. Judicial review is consistent with the legislative sovereignty of Parliament. The court's purpose in judicial review proceedings is to ensure that public bodies substantively and procedurally exercise their powers in the way in which Parliament intended. Answer [D] is correct. Answers [A] and [B] are incorrect because the constitutional role of British judges is not to question an Act of Parliament but to give effect to it. Answer [C] is incorrect. Judicial review is often concerned with matters of considerable political significance.

10. Answer [A], the requirement under O. 53 that applications for judicial review should be begun within 3 months was cited by Lord Diplock, as was answer [B], the 'filter' role played by the leave procedure to prevent vexatious litigation being directed against public bodies. Lord Diplock also recognised the procedural inadequacies of the 'old' judicial review proceedings, answer [D]. Answer [C] is the correct answer in that Lord Diplock recognised that it was appropriate for public bodies to have civil remedies awarded against them. Under the reformed O. 53 proceedings it was possible to claim the civil law remedies of damages, declaration and injunction as well as the public law prerogative orders.

11. Lord Diplock's judgment in *O'Reilly* v *Mackman* [1983] 2 AC 237, established the general rule about proceedings against public bodies being commenced under RSC O. 53. Certain exceptions to the 'exclusivity rule' were recognised where an action commenced by a writ or an originating summons would be allowed. Answers [A], [B] and [C] are situations which may fall outside of the 'exclusivity' rule. Answer [D] would not, because under the 'reformed' O. 53 proceedings damages could be claimed against public bodies in judicial review proceedings and could not be commenced by way of writ or originating summons.

12. In most cases it will be clear whether an organisation can be considered to be a 'public body' and therefore susceptible to judicial review. The *Datafin* case provides some guidance as to the factors the court considers when determining if an organisation is a public body. Answers [A] and [B] indicate that where an organisation is created or empowered under statute or the prerogative, it raises the presumption of it being a public body. The same principle is applied to answer [C], where the body takes decisions which affect the public. Answer [D] is the correct answer in the context of *Datafin*. The Court of Appeal considered that the Panel on Take-overs and Mergers to be susceptible to review because there were no other means by which those affected by the Panel's decisions could challenge those decisions.

13. Answer [A] is the correct answer. A City Technical College, a non-fee paying publically funded institution is a matter of public law. Answer [B] is not a public body: see *Law* v *National Greyhound Racing*

Club Ltd [1983] 3 All ER 300. Answer [C] is not a public body: see *R v Governors of Haberdashers' Aske's Hatcham College Trust, ex parte T, The Times*, 19 October 1994. Answer [D] is not a public body: see *R v Disciplinary Committee of the Jockey Club, ex parte Aga Khan* [1993] 2 All ER 853.

14. The criteria for granting *locus standi* is a problematic area of judicial review especially where the applicant is a pressure group. The issue of *locus standi* is a mixed question of law and fact and decided on a case by case basis. Two recent decisions – *R v Secretary of State for the Environment, ex parte Greenpeace* [1994] 1 WLR 570 CA and *R v Secretary of State for Foreign Affairs, ex parte World Development Movement Ltd* [1995] 1 All ER 611 will provide some guidance when advising SET. The absence of any other group or person to challenge the decision [D] is incorrect, as per *World Development Movement* is clearly in SET's favour as are answers [C] and [A] especially, according to *Greenpeace*, the number of local activists affected directly by the decision as opposed to the size SET's national membership. Answer [B] is correct and could be held against finding *locus standi* referred to in *Greenpeace* and see the House of Lords in *IRC v National Federation of Self-Employed and Small Businesses Ltd* [1982] AC 617.

15. Since 1977, RSC O. 53 requires that an application must be received within 3 months from the date of the decision complained of (RSC O. 53, r. 4); that a completed application on form 86A and a sworn affidavit verifying the facts must be filed at the High Court; and more importantly, that at leave stage the applicant must be able to show that he has sufficient interest in the case, or *locus standi* (see *O'Reilly v Mackman* [1983] 2 AC 237 and *Inland Revenue Commissioners v National Federation of Self-Employed and Small Businesses* [1982] AC 617); also that he has a ground for judicial review, that is, has an arguable case and thus is not 'frivolous' or 'vexatious'. Answers [A], [B] and [D] are incorrect. Answer [C] is correct by indicating the steps that Andrew must take to be successful at the 'leave' stage.

16. Lord Diplock's classification of the substantive grounds of judicial review in the *GCHQ* case provides a starting point to understand this difficult area of law. Two points should always be borne in mind about Lord Diplock's approach. First, it is not a universally acknowledged categorisation and many textbooks use different terminologies such as procedural and substantive *ultra vires*. Secondly, the substantive grounds are not discreet. In practice there is a considerable degree of overlap between each. For the purposes of question 16, answer [A] correctly identifies the substantive grounds of judicial review. Answer [B], [C] and [D] are incorrect.

17. In *Council of Civil Service Unions* v *Minister for the Civil Service* [1985] AC 374 (the *GCHQ* case), Lord Diplock described 'irrationality' as a substantive ground of judicial review in preference to the traditional '*Wednesbury* unreasonableness'. Whilst each of the substantive grounds suffers from terminological uncertainty, the parameters of irrationality appear to be as ambiguous as any. Answer [D] comes within the boundaries of irrationality as it reflects Lord Greene's classic statement of 'unreasonableness' in *Associated Provincial Picture Houses Ltd* v *Wednesbury Corporation* [1948] 1 KB 223. Answers [B] and [C] also come within the concept of irrationality: see Lord Denning's comments in *Hall and Co. Ltd* v *Shoreham by Sea Urban District Council* [1964] 1 WLR 240. Answer [A], where the decision maker has failed to follow the correct procedure, would come within the ground of procedural improprietory and is the correct answer.

18. Answer [A] is incorrect. Even where statutory powers are silent on a particular point, public bodies will not be given a complete discretion as to how they conduct themselves. The courts will impose the common law rules of natural justice on the decision-making process. For example, there is a requirement that public bodies should act fairly: see *Re HK (an infant)* [1967] 2 QB 617. Answer [B] is incorrect. In the absence of statutory provisions there is generally no right to have an oral hearing: see *Selvarajan* v *Race Relations Board* [1976] 1 All ER 12. Answer [C] is also incorrect. Barry is not automatically entitled to legal representation: see *Maynard* v *Osmond* [1977] QB 240. Answer [D] is correct. A person's entitlement to make representations is dependent upon the circumstances of each case. As Barry's livelihood, pension entitlement etc. is at stake, he will almost certainly be entitled to make representations.

19. For guidance on this question see *R* v *Somerset County Council, ex parte Fewings* [1995] 1 WLR 1037. Answer [A] is incorrect. Parliament has not given the minister complete discretion. The powers can only be used for a direct or incidental purpose as provided for by Parliament. Answer [B] is incorrect. The minister cannot exercise powers under s. 2 *per se* on the basis of moral considerations; although see the dissenting judgment of Simon Brown LJ in the *Somerset* case. Answer [D] is also incorrect. Answer [C] is correct. In order to act lawfully, the minister would have to show how the moral issues were conducive to the purpose of the legislation. If it could be proven that they were, it would be permissible for them to be taken into account.

20. For guidance on this question see *R* v *Secretary of State for the Home Department, ex parte Silva and another, The Times*, 1 April 1994. Answer [A] is incorrect. The doctrine of legitimate expectation does not arise automatically. Answers [C] and [D] are also incorrect, as the doctrine is not automatically excluded in these circumstances. Answer [B] is the correct answer. Carlos would have to prove that to allow the Home Secretary to change his original decision would be unfair or detrimental to good administration: see *Attorney-General of Hong Kong* v *Ng Yuen Shiu* [1983] 2 AC 629.

21. Local authorities are created and empowered by statute. Every action taken therefore cannot be *ultra vires* the powers Parliament has given to them. In order to determine the question of whether Anytown District Council has acted lawfully, it is necessary to consider the powers the authority is purporting to act under. Clearly the insurance scheme is not expressly authorised. However, it will be lawful if Anytown can prove it to be reasonably incidental to s. 34 of the Council Housing Act 1989. Case law would suggest that it is: see *Attorney-General* v *Crayford UDC* [1962] Ch 575. Answer [A] is correct and answers [B], [C] and [D] are incorrect.

22. The question involves a fundamental principle of English public law. Answer [D] is correct. The imposition of the charge is not reasonably incidental to the council's statutory powers but it is well established since the Bill of Rights 1689 that no charge can be levied on the public unless there is express statutory authority. No such authority exists under the fictitious Act. Therefore answers [A], [B] and [C] are incorrect.

23. Answer [D] is correct. Although there is a presumption against legislation having retrospective effect, the courts will recognise and enforce such legislation where it appears expressly or by implication to have been the intention of the legislature. That principle clearly applies in this situation: see the speech of Willes J in *Phillips* v *Eyre* (1870) LR 6 QB 1, 23. Answers [A], [B] and [C] are incorrect.

24. The rule against bias is one of the most strictly applied of all judicial principles relating to natural justice. There are two tests for bias: where there is a reasonable suspicion of bias and where there is a real likelihood of bias. Where a body is exercising a judicial function, the reasonable suspicion test is appropriate: see *R* v *Sussex Justices, ex parte McCarthy* [1924] 1 KB 256 and *R* v *Liverpool Justices, ex parte Topping* [1993] 1 WLR 119. It will be sufficient for Erika to show whether a reasonable and fair minded person, who knew all the facts, would have a reasonable suspicion that Erika did not receive a fair trial. Answer [A] is incorrect. It is not necessary for Erika to show actual bias. Answers [B] and [C] are also incorrect. Answer [D] is correct.

25. For guidance on this question see *R* v *Ministry of Defence, ex parte Smith* [1996] 2 WLR 305. Answer [D] is incorrect. The Court of Appeal in Smith expressly declared it to be a justiciable issue. Answer [C] is also incorrect. In *Smith* the relationship between the administrative discharge and the European Convention was not directly addressed, although the Master of the Rolls did suggest that failure by a decision maker to make reference to the Convention when making a decision was not, in itself, a ground for review. Answer [B] is incorrect because the Court of Appeal was of the opinion that irrationality could not apply to a measure that had been approved by both Houses of Parliament. On the basis of the decision in *Smith*, answer [A] is correct.

26. For guidance on this answer see *R* v *Higher Education Funding Council, ex parte Institute of Dental Surgery* [1994] 1 All ER 651. Answer [A] is incorrect. There is no such general duty. Answers [C] and [D] are also incorrect. Answer [B], according to the decision in *Higher Education Funding*, is correct. Such cases would include where the decision involves the personal liberty of the applicant or where the way in which the decision has been made appears aberrant.

27. Answer [A] is a legislative attempt to exclude the court's jurisdiction. A finality clause seeks to make the decision of the public body non-reviewable. Answers [C] and [D] are also legislative clauses which seek to oust the review jurisdiction of the courts. In practice 'as if enacted' and 'conclusive evidence' clauses attempt to achieve the same result to protect the exercise of delegated legislative powers from review. A 'time limits' clause, answer [B], is correct because it is not an ouster clause, although it may have a similar effect. Legislation may indicate a time limit when any decision made under those powers can be questioned. For an illustration of the principle: see *Smith* v *East Elloe District Council* [1956] AC 736. Many of the above attempts to exclude the jurisdiction of the courts completely have proven unsuccessful.

28. The principle established by answer [A] was decided by the *Council of Civil Service Unions* v *Minister for the Civil Service* [1984] 3 WLR 1174. The principle established by answer [D] was decided by *Conway* v *Rimmer* [1968] AC 610. Answer [B] was established before *Anisiminic*; it reflects a basic principle of judicial review that where a public body acts in error within the jurisdiction that Parliament has granted, it will be acting *ultra vires* and the decision can be quashed by an order for *certiorari*. *Anisminic* therefore established the principle in answer [C].

29. It was suggested in 1987, by the Head of the Home Civil Service, Sir Robert Armstrong, that civil servants have a duty 'to provide the Government of the day with advice on the formulation of the policies of the Government, and to manage and deliver the services for which the Government is responsible'. Answer [A] is incorrect. Ministers are directly responsible to Parliament. Answers [B] and [C] are also incorrect. A civil servant's duty lies therefore to the departmental minister. Answer [D] is correct.

30. A lack of public awareness is a criticism that is consistently made against the Parliamentary Commissioner compared to similar bodies in other jurisdictions. Answers [B], [C] and [D] are incorrect. In 1994, 1,322 complaints were referred to the Parliamentary Commissioner which represented a dramatic increase on the 986 complaints referred in 1993. Answer [A] is correct.

31. Answer [A] is correctly ascribed to the office of the Parliamentary Commissioner. Complaints must be in writing and made through an MP. Answer [B] is also correctly ascribed. Schedule 2 of the 1967 Act lays down those Departments which are subject to the Commissioner's jurisdiction. Answer [C] is also correct. Even where a matter falls within the PCA's jurisdiction, s. 5(5) of the 1967 Act allows the Commissioner a discretion whether to accept the complaint or not. Answer [D] is therefore the answer you need. It incorrectly ascribes to the PCA the power to grant a remedy and award compensation in cases where maladministration has been found.

32. Susan is entitled to seek judicial review against the way in which the Commissioner has exercised his statutory powers. Answers [A], [B] and [C] are incorrect. Following *R v Parliamentary Commissioner for Administration, ex parte Dyer* [1994] 1 All ER 375, the office of the PCA is susceptible to review, although given the breadth of the discretion conferred on the PCA by Parliament, the courts are reluctant to intervene. Answer [D] is correct.

33. The concept of 'maladministration' is central to the PCA's jurisdiction. Although referred to in ss. 5(1)(a) and 10(3) of the Parliamentary Commissioner Act 1967, maladministration is not defined. A starting point in deciding whether 'maladministration' has occurred is by reference to the Crossman catalogue. Richard Crossman, who was instrumental in securing the passage of the Bill though Parliament, defined maladministration as 'bias, neglect, inattention, delay, incompetence, ineptitude, perversity, turpitude, arbitrariness. Answers [A], [B] and [D] correctly identify elements from the Crossman catalogue. Answer [C] cites characteristics of decision making which are not cited in the catalogue, and is therefore the correct answer. For a more up-to-date explanation of the principles of maladministration see the PCA's Annual Report to Parliament in 1993.

34. A trend in administrative accountability during the last 30 years has been the growth of ombudsmen covering a wide range of activities by public bodies. The word 'ombudsman' is Swedish and means representative of the people. The Swedish ombudsman was established in 1809. Following the introduction of the Parliamentary Commissioner in 1967, answer [A], the Parliamentary Commissioner for Standards was established in 1995, answer [B], the Legal Services Commissioner in 1990 and answer [C], the European Community ombudsman in 1992. Answer [D] does not hold office and is the correct answer.

35. The Parliamentary Commissioner for Administration forms part of the political element of administrative accountability. Answer [C] is correct and answers [A], [B], and [D] are incorrect.

36. The UK is not a federal state and answer [B] is incorrect. The relationship between central and local government is not based upon the principle of subsidiarity, answer [C], nor does local government exercise its functions as a 'quasi governmental' body, answer [D]. Answer A is correct. Central government devolves to local government by legislation, its administrative powers and duties. The important characteristic of a devolved or delegated system is that ultimate control (sovereignty) rests with the central authority, Parliament, and can legally be withdrawn from local government at any time.

37. The Widdicombe Committee identified the merits of local government as being, answer [A] responsive to local needs, answer [C] participatory, through local democracy and answer [D], pluralistic, in that the system of local government contributes to the national political system. Answer [B], the accountability function, was not identified by Widdicombe and is the correct answer.

38. The structure and functions of local government are almost exclusively the creation of statute, for example, the Local Government Act 1972 and the Local Government and Housing Act 1989. Increasingly, European Community law is imposing legal obligations on local authorities and therefore answer [D] correctly identifies the legal source of local government powers and answers [A], [B] and [C] are incorrect.

39. Apart from the increasing influence of European Community law, the legal powers and duties of local government are exclusively conferred by statute. Local authorities are therefore subject to the *ultra vires* doctrine to ensure they exercise their substantive and procedural powers lawfully. Although curtailed by Conservative Governments since 1979, statement (i) correctly recognises that local government raises finance through taxation, for example, the poll tax was established by the Local Government Finance Act 1992. Local government also exercises important functions in strategic planning and planning control (statement (ii)). Statement (iii) correctly identifies that local government has an important law-making function. Acting under the authority of the Acts of Parliament, councils make by-laws. Statement (iv) correctly recognises that local authorities exercise important licensing and regulatory roles, for example, the granting of taxi licences or the approval of child care facilities. Answer [D] is correct.

40. The structure of local government has been substantially revised on several occasions during the last 25 years, most notably by the Local Government Acts of 1972 and 1985. Answer [A] is the correct answer. Six Metropolitan County Councils were created by the Local Government Act 1972 but were abolished by the Local Government Act 1985 with effect from 1 April 1986. Metropolitan District Councils and Non-Metropolitan Districts (answers [B] and [D]), established under the 1972 Act, still exist. From 1 April 1996, certain areas of local government have been administered under a Unitary Council (answer[C]); a local authority which combines the traditional functions of both District and County Councils.

41. The delegation of some legislative powers by Parliament to subordinate public bodies is a practical manifestation of the complex demands on the government of a modern state such as the UK. Delegated legislation is therefore justified by a number of reasons. Answer [A] correctly recognises that Parliament doesn't have the time to enact every piece of legislation. Delegating its law-making powers in carefully defined areas is an efficient use of legislative time. Answer [B] recognises that delegated legislation suited to enacting law on technical subject-matter, which requires consultation with interested bodies, could not be meaningfully debated by Parliament. Answer [D] recognises that delegated legislation provides flexibility, in that it can be used for bringing into effect or amending primary legislation and can be applied to emergency situations. Answer [C] is therefore not an acceptable reason for Parliament delegating its legislative powers.

42. Parliament is legislatively sovereign in that it can delegate its law-making powers for whatever purpose and effect Parliament considers appropriate. However, there is a presumption that delegated legislation should not be used for answer [B], matters of general principle, as this may be considered as posing a threat to Parliamentary government. There is also a presumption that the legislative powers should not be sub-delegated, although Parliament may expressly authorise sub-delegation where appropriate, for example, the Emergency Powers (Defence) Act 1939. Answer [D] recognises a further presumption that legislation, whether primary or delegated should not be retrospective in operation, although once again Parliament may express the desire that legislation should have retrospective effect. Answer [A] is the correct answer. Delegated legislation is one of the major ways by which Community law is received into the domestic law of the UK. For example, the European Communities Act 1972 confers on the government wide legislative powers to make Orders-in-Council and ministerial regulations.

43. The Statutory Instruments Act 1946 establishes the procedural framework by which the forms of delegated legislation covered by the Act come into effect. Answer [A], Statutory Orders in Council are subject to the 1946 Act and must be distinguished from Prerogative Orders in Council which are not. Answers [C] and [D] correctly recognise that delegated legislation, made under the 1946 Act, can be known by a variety of names: rules and orders. Answer [B] is the correct answer. Although the Immigration Rules are a form of subordinate legislation, they are made under the authority of the Immigration Act 1971 and not the 1946 Act.

44. One of the main protections against the abuse of delegated legislative powers by public bodies is through judicial review. Answer [C] correctly states the validity of primary legislation cannot be questioned by the courts. Answer [D] correctly identifies that whilst Parliament may delegate exceptionally wide powers, it would be most unlikely to delegate absolute substantive or procedural powers. Answer [A] correctly identifies that delegated legislation, as a matter of policy will usually deal with 'justiciable' issues and therefore be susceptible to the judicial review. Answer [B] is the answer you need. Judicial review can be excluded by Parliament, by an ouster clause. For the courts to recognise such a clause there would have to be a clear, unambiguous intention on the face of the parent Act.

45. In determining the legality of the exercise of delegated legislative powers by public bodies, the courts will apply the following approach. Answer [B] recognises the court will refer to the parent Act or enabling legislation to determine whether the public body has exercised the substantive and/or procedural powers within the terms prescribed by Parliament. Answer [D] recognises the courts will impose the common-law principles of natural justice on the exercise of the delegated powers. Answer [A] recognises the direct and pervasive influence of European Community law. It is now well established that the English courts must give effect to Community law when interpreting primary and secondary legislation. Answer [C] is the correct answer. The Convention has only a presumptive effect and in the important recent decision of R v Ministry of Defence, ex parte Smith [1996] 2 WLR 305, the Master of the Rolls suggested that failure by the decision maker to consider the effects of the Convention would not be a ground upon which a decision could be challenged.

46. The Joint Committee comprises 7 members from the House of Commons and 7 from the House of Lords and examines approximately 1,000 instruments during a Parliamentary session. Some of the grounds on which the Committee will report to Parliament are: answer [A] where the instrument is to operate retrospectively; answer [B] where the parent Act excludes review by the courts; and answer [C] where the instrument imposes a tax. Answer [D] is the correct answer. Where an instrument gives effect to Community law, is not, by itself, a reason for the Committee to make a report to Parliament.

47. Parliament delegates law-making powers to a wide range of 'public bodies' including answer [A] judges in the form of the Rules of the Supreme Court; answer [C] the Nature Conservancy Council; and answer [D] local authorities to make by-laws. Answer [B], the universities do not have delegated law-making powers conferred on them by Parliament.

48. A question which should indicate to you the extent to which delegated legislation in general and statutory instruments in particular are applied to keep the modern state apparatus functioning. In 1995 there were approximately 3,000 statutory instruments passed. Answer [B] is correct and answers [A], [C] and [D] incorrect.

49. The Franks Committee 1957 identified that most statutory tribunals exercise an adjudicatory function as opposed to being part of the administration, answer [B], exercising a review function, answer [C] or exercising a supervisory jurisdiction, answer [D]. Answer [A] is the correct answer.

50. The reasons put forward justifying a system of administrative tribunals are based as much on practical considerations as any other. Answer [A] recognises tribunals can be justified in that they adopt informal procedurals, the strict rules of evidence do not apply and seek to encourage public accessibility. Answer [C] recognises that many tribunals require the specialist knowledge of its members to make decisions. Answer [D] also recognises that tribunals are better suited than courts to implement social policy. Answer [B] therefore is the correct answer. It would clearly pose a threat to the constitutional principle of the rule of law if the powers of appointment and tenure of tribunal members were not impartial, based on merit and controlled by government departments.

51. When establishing a statutory scheme of state regulation or social security provision, Parliament will recognise that disputes about the way in which the legal and administrative powers are exercised will inevitably arise. There are various ways by which these disputes can be adjudicated. A specialist tribunal could be established as in answer [A]. Answer [B] correctly recognises that the jurisdiction of the County Court (or any other ordinary court) could be extended. A Welfare Benefits Ombudsman could be established as in answer [D]. Answer [C] is therefore the least appropriate form of accountability; although administratively permissible, it would be inappropriate for the Welfare Benefits Agency to adjudicate in disputes between its own decisions and the public.

52. Tribunals in administrative law have the following characteristics: they have a limited jurisdiction; their errors of law are subject to judicial review and contrary to popular belief, the procedure is adversarial, in that when making its decision the tribunal should hear both sides of the case, and should decide between them without conducting an inquiry of its own. Answer [B] is therefore correct and answers [A], [C] and [D] are incorrect.

53. In determining whether a tribunal can be categorised as an inferior court, the identification of certain characteristics raises the presumption that the tribunal is an inferior court within the meaning of RSC O. 52, r. 1(2)(iii). Answers [B], [C] and [D] are indicative of such a status. Answer [A] is not. For example, according to the decision in *Peach Grey & Co. (A Firm)* v *Sommers* [1995] 2 All ER 513 an industrial tribunal was held to be an inferior court. Industrial tribunals determine employment law disputes between employers and employees, the vast majority of whom operate in the private and not the public sector.

54. According to the Franks Report 1957, public inquiries fulfil two functions. First, they protect the interests of the public, enabling their views to be heard in favour or against proposals by public bodies. Secondly, to ensure that public officials are fully informed about issues and relevant public opinion when making a decision. It is obviously in the interests of natural justice that certain procedural rules should be established for inquiries to follow. The source of the procedural rules are each of those listed: answer [B] s. 9 of the Tribunals and Inquiries Act 1992, answer [C] recognises that inquiries will be subject to the common-law principles of natural justice and answer [D] that the Lord Chancellor may, after consulting the Council on Tribunals, make procedural rules regulating the conduct of inquiries. Answer [A] is correct.

55. Answer [B] is incorrect. Parliamentary privilege does not apply. Answers [C] and [D] are also incorrect. Whilst the Crown Proceedings Act 1947 enabled the Crown to be sued in tort and contract, it has only recently been established in *M* v *Home Office* [1993] 3 WLR 433 that injunctive relief can be ordered against a minister of the Crown. Answer [A] is correct.

56. Until Parliament passed the Crown Proceedings Act 1947, the general proposition was that the Crown was not liable to civil actions.

Crown immunity extended to liability in tort but it had long been recognised that it should be possible to obtain judicial redress to enforce a contractual obligation against the Crown or a government minister under the petition of right. Section 1 of the 1947 Act, however, puts the Crown in the same position as other defendants in respect of civil liability including the enforcement of contracts. Answer [A] is incorrect. Answer [B] is also incorrect. The Petition of Right Act 1860 provided a remedy to enforce the Crown's contractual liabilities before the Crown Proceedings Act and was repealed by the 1947 legislation. Answer [D] does not apply either as Sonia was acting within the scope of her ostensible authority. Answer [C] is correct. The Crown is liable to fulfil its obligations under the contract as any other party would be.

57. Answer [A] is incorrect. Whilst estoppel is a private law doctrine it is recognised in public law, although not in the circumstances suggested by answer [B]. Answer [C] is also incorrect. Answer [D] is the correct answer. Whilst the doctrine will not be applied to prevent a public authority from fulfilling its public duties or powers, *Western Fish* established that estoppel would apply in two situations. First, where the person to whom the representations had been made thought the representor had authority to bind the public body and there had been a lawful delegation of power. Secondly, where the public body waived a particular formality, it would be estopped from relying upon the lack of formality.

58. In terms of their employment rights, Raymond should be advised that Crown servants occupy a special contractual position. At common law, the Crown can dismiss its servants at its pleasure. Therefore Raymond has no right to sue for wrongful dismissal in the County Court. Answers [B] and [C] are incorrect. Raymond should be advised however that he will be entitled to commence an action for unfair dismissal at an industrial tribunal. This right was granted to Crown Servants in 1971. Answer [A] is correct and answer [D] incorrect.

59. It is often necessary for parties to litigation to inspect documents in the possession or control of their opponents. There are some circumstances, however, where a public body can claim that it is not in the public interest for a document or a class of documents to be disclosed to the other side. This 'privilege' is now known as 'public interest immunity'. The courts have developed substantive and procedural principles as to how the privilege can be claimed. Answer [D] is the correct answer. The decision in *Conway* v *Rimmer* [1968] AC 910 forms the basis of the modern law of public interest immunity. Answers [A], [B] and [C] are incorrect.

60. The importance of PII is growing in both civil and criminal cases. Answers [A] and [B] are therefore incorrect. Despite views to the contrary held by the Attorney General, Sir Nicholas Lyell (see the Scott Report), answer [C] is also incorrect. Answer [D] correctly recognises the principles of PII are subject to distinctive approaches based on civil and criminal cases as per *R* v *Chief Constable of the West Midlands Police, ex parte Wiley* [1994] 3 All ER 420.

TITLES IN THE SERIES

Test Yourself in Constitutional & Administrative Law
Test Yourself in Contract
Test Yourself in Company Law
Test Yourself in Conveyancing
Test Yourself in Wills & Probate
Test Yourself in EC Law